Then They Leave Home

Parenting After the Kids Grow Up

BONI PIPER & JUDITH BALSWICK

InterVarsity Press
Downers Grove, Illinois

InterVarsity Press® is the book-publishing division of InterVarsity Christian Fellowship®, a student movement active on campus at hundreds of universities, colleges and schools of nursing in the United States of America, and a member movement of the International Fellowship of Evangelical Students. For information about local and regional activities, write Public Relations Dept., InterVarsity Christian Fellowship, 6400 Schroeder Rd., P.O. Box 7895, Madison, WI 53707-7895.

Scripture quotations, unless otherwise noted, are from the New Revised Standard Version of the Bible, copyright 1989 by the Division of Christian Education of the National Council of the Churches of Christ in the USA. Used by permission. All rights reserved.

"Circumplex Model of Family Systems," David H. Olson, Ph.D., Family Social Service Department of the University of Minnesota. Used by permission. All rights reserved.

Cover photograph: Stock Market, Nancy Santullo, 1996

ISBN 0-8308-1964-9

Printed in the United States of America ∞

Library of Congress Cataloging-in-Publication Data

Piper, Boni.
    Then they leave home: parenting after the kids grow up/Boni
  Piper & Judith Balswick
        p.   cm.
    Includes bibliographical references.
    ISBN 0-8308-1964-9 (alk. paper)
    1. Parent and adult child.   2. Autonomy in youth.
  3. Intergenerational relations.   4. Adult children living with
  parents.   5. Life cycle, Human—Religious aspects—Christianity.
  I. Balswick, Judith K.   II. Title.
  HQ755.86.P56   1997
  306.874—dc21   97-12915
                                                                    CIP

19	18	17	16	15	14	13	12	11	10	9	8	7	6	5	4	3	2	1
12	11	10	09	08	07	06	05	04	03	02	01	00	99	98	97			

To Aaron, Karlie & Sarah

Jacque & Joel

children & friends

Acknowledgments

We are grateful for the opportunity to write again with each other. We particularly want to thank Rodney Clapp, our editor, for his faith in our work and his constant positive feedback. We feel blessed to work with you, Rodney.

We thank Don and Jack for their consistent encouragement and for their loving partnership in the letting-go process.

We are grateful to clients and friends who have allowed us to share their stories in this book. And for our children, who have consented to be vulnerable in print with us, we praise God.

1

Leaving Home

······························

How well I (Boni) remember the pain I felt the day we left our oldest child, Aaron, at college, three thousand miles from our home, and began the drive home without him. My husband and I said little during the first five hundred miles as our two daughters chattered in the back seat, trying to cheer us up and restore the joy in our cross-country vacation trip. We were glad for their efforts, but nothing could take away the pain of not having our son with us. So on we drove, sightseeing, picnicking, swimming and laughing, all with an underlying sense of loss so deep that we ached.

Later, as I talked about this pain with a friend, she asked if I had not wanted Aaron to go to college. Or was it the school he chose that upset me? Was I fearful that something would happen to him in the East? No, I said again and again: I had never realized it would hurt so much. I am sure she never understood what was wrong with me or why I had such a reaction.

Two years later, making the same trip after leaving our son and elder daughter at the same school, the ache returned. But this time *two* of them were gone! Stopping at a friend's home on our way back to Seattle, we talked of the loss I felt and the pain of missing our children. "It's awful, isn't it?" my friend said knowingly. "Somebody should have told us about this time in a parent's life!" How I agreed, and I was blessed to hear someone echo my feelings.

In this anguish I have often had another thought, one that amused me: What if they didn't go? That would be a different kind of anguish, perhaps one even greater than what I was feeling. I had wanted everything to stay the same: for the children to be children forever, for us to be a family forever.

How glad I am now that God does not take all our thoughts and fears too seriously and give us what we think we want. Having gone through the leaving process with two of our three children, I am enjoying immensely having adult children with their own ideas and goals for life. How glad I am to see their independence, to hear of their dreams and adventures and to see them used in God's kingdom. This joy is at least as great as the earlier pain.

Being Left Behind

In the Balswick family, Jack and I (Judy) were in the unusual situation of leaving our daughter behind after she graduated from high school. We were both offered positions at a seminary twenty-five hundred miles from our home. Earlier Jacque had decided to attend the university in our hometown, so it was she who bade us goodby that summer.

Jacque looked forlorn as we packed our household and sold the home she had lived in during her high-school years. It was as if fate had played a dirty trick on us. This was twisted and turned around, for I had always imagined it would be she who packed her things to head off to college. Much to my chagrin, we were leaving her behind, and that didn't set right with me. But there she was, standing at the drive waving goodby to us.

I can still see her standing there and remember how my heart sank as I tried to take in the circumstances that had unexpectedly changed our plans. Although I knew she had a good support system of friends and church community, I still felt my husband and I had betrayed her in some way. She too remembers how vulnerable she felt knowing that her family and her home were taken from her, so to speak. Her security was gone. She was not going to be included in this part of our family story. It felt strangely cruel and unnatural. From now on she would be visiting us on unknown territory. There was a feeling of dread in my heart, and I wondered how we were going to manage through this stage of our lives.

The other part of the story, of course, is that Jacque was eager to be on her own. She was excited to be going to the university, staying in the dorm and enjoying the freedom of living on her own. I know she was not feeling nearly as bad as I was feeling. There was sadness and uncertainty, but it was tempered with anticipation and the clarity of her choice. We each had mixed emotions. We each had our personal journey to go through during these leaving-home years.

Unfeathering the Nest

Some parents have felt completely different about this time of life than we did. Marsha and Tom longed for the day when Peter left for school. It wasn't that they didn't love Peter or that they did not enjoy parenting him. But they were ready to move on to the next stage and to focus on their marriage. Both Tom and Marsha had flourishing careers and were eager to develop them without the conflicts that accompany parenting. When Peter began to prepare to live on his own, they found ways of encouraging the move.

Peter wanted to move home after a four-year stint in a local college. "No way!" responded his parents, as they had already rented his room to an exchange student. Peter tried everything to convince them he was not ready to make it on his own. He had no job, no money and no place to live. Marsha and Tom held firm. They believed he needed to delve into his inner resources to face the challenges of growing up. They sympathized with his fears and insecurity but insisted he could manage on his own.

Peter got a job in a local restaurant and arranged to live with some good friends. Maturity came to him through what seemed at the time to be harsh reality. In fact Tom and Marsha had had parents who held a similar philosophy of life. They understood how experience can be the very thing that gives a young person the confidence to make it on his or her own. They were persuaded that unfeathering the nest was the best thing they could do for their adult child.

The Leaving-Home Day

The leaving-home day is a momentous event that marks a beginning as well as an ending of life as it has been. It takes into account the past that is already behind, the present that is full of ambiguity and the future that holds the secret to what will be. This ritual acknowledges a physical and an emotional change but also a change in attitude and perspective for both parents and children. It is a time when disparate emotions, sadness and gladness, can be expressed at the same time. It is the making of something new: a child becomes an adult. It marks a significant rite of passage. Whether the goodby ritual is a simple handshake, a wink, a smile, a shed tear, a hug, a turned head or an angry statement, it is a gesture that symbolizes the end and a beginning.

I (Judy) remember vividly my leaving-home day. Although I had been attending college away from home for two years, the significant leaving came near the end of that time. I think of sitting on my suitcases in an empty dorm room, looking out the window with tears streaming down my face and watching my parents drive away from campus with all my stuff. I had just finished the second year at my denominational college in Chicago, and I was on my way to visit my boyfriend in California. I was aware of my excitement and my fear of being on my own. I had made a choice to spend the summer with Jack's family and pursue a relationship that would likely lead to marriage. I had a clear sense that I was leaving my parents to join a new family. I believed I was making the right decision, and I was ready to face the consequences of my own choices in life. I was ready to be on my own but at the same time felt vulnerable and unsure.

The leaving day announces to the world that adult children are on their own in ways they never before experienced. Even though parents may still provide in financial and emotional ways, young adults are now responsible in a new way for the choices they make about their lives. Parents hope for the best as they watch their adult children embark on their venture of independence, whether it be a new job, further schooling, military service, marriage or travel. Whatever happens from this day, for better or worse, parents are no longer in the driver's seat.

Watching from the back seat of your young adult's life will take some doing. There is a need to trust the inexperienced driver, and there will be some anxious moments. Fathers may respond differently from mothers. Cultural values will influence how much the back-seat drivers will be involved. Other factors, such as the number of children in a family, sibling order, the number of parents in the back seat or a blended or extended family system, will influence the transition from front to back seat. Beliefs about leaving home will also affect the smoothness of the ride. Whether we let them drive away with our blessing, our reservation or our curse, this time-honored ritual has set things in motion.

Developing a Vision

The letting-go process starts far earlier than when our children are eighteen or twenty-one years old. "Leaving home is the logical extension of the formation of a self that begins at birth" (Anderson and Mitchell 1993:40). As we look at our newborn children, we imagine them as adult world leaders or healers or have other lofty expectations. In those early moments of fantasy, we dream dreams for our children that take them to wonderful and exotic places, that give them important lives to live and enormous purposes to fulfill. The reality that they will have to leave us in order to do those great and marvelous works is not fully realized. Surely they will always be here, looking into our eyes and knowing we have the answers to all their problems.

But in order for the dreams that we dream for our children, as well as those they dream for themselves, to become reality, they need to become their own persons. And this knowledge of their own strength and potency begins or fails fairly early in life. When our children are aware that leaving not only is permitted but also is part of the plan of God for their lives as well as ours, they look forward to a life of their own that feels productive and full. Unfortunately this is not what we always communicate.

In chapter two we will look more closely at the developmental perspective of leaving home. As we grasp the process from beginning to end and see the specific tasks delegated to the young adult at this time, we will be more prepared to participate in a positive way to their leaving.

The Leaving Process
Children go about leaving home in many different ways. Some ways are healthier than others, of course, but most get the job done. Herbert Anderson and Kenneth Mitchell have described a number of ways this can happen in *Leaving Home* (1993:2-20). Some examples from these categories follow.

1. *Leaving without its being noticed.* In this leaving there is no acknowledgment of the leaving process. A child moves out, and no one marks the move as significant. It could be thought of as a silent leaving in that no one notices or pays attention.

Carla's leaving was like that. In high school she began spending more and more time with her friends and less time with her single mom. When she was sixteen, she moved in with her boyfriend. She remembers no conversation with her mother regarding the move. There was no acknowledgment of the implications of this in their relationship or on Carla's life. She was not sure her mom cared that she was gone.

2. *The hidden departure.* This leaving happens without the parents' knowledge. Perhaps a child eloped or joined the military without informing anyone about the decision. It is a sneaky kind of leaving since the family is informed after the fact. Garrison Keillor tells about the hidden departure of Dale, a graduate of Lake Wobegon High School, class of 1986. The day after graduation Dale announced to his

mother that he had joined the navy.

"Why so soon?" his mother said. . . . "Honey. You didn't. Oh Dale. How could you do this? Honey, you don't even know how to swim. You'd be out in the ocean someplace."

"Ma, they carry life preservers."

"How do you know that?"

"It's the law. They have to."

"Who's going to enforce it?" (Keillor 1987:66)

This worried parent had no warning and put up the only protest she could.

3. *The angry leaving.* Blaming can play a big role in this leaving. Sometimes the child blames the parents for his or her unhappiness ("You people drive me crazy!"), or possibly the parents blame their child for disrupting the family ("You're impossible to live with!"), and out the child goes.

This leaving usually takes place after much conflict between parents and the young adult. Because they are unable to resolve their differences, the fighting escalates, and separation appears to be the only way out of strife. Natalie left her home in a huff. There was so much disruption she felt the only thing to do was to get out of her tumultuous household. Both she and her parents blamed each other for her abrupt departure.

4. *The pretended leaving.* This leaving is a ploy. The parents are still in the driver's seat. Even though the adult child physically leaves home, he or she is still treated like a child and remains emotionally dependent on the parents. It may look like leaving, but no real changes have been made.

Gary was the last of four children. When he moved into his own apartment, it seemed like a natural thing to do. His parents were excited for him, and his mother had lots of ideas of how to fix up the place. She brought him items for his kitchen, cooked meals to put in his freezer and even sneaked in to clean the place every now and then. His father called friends to check on how Gary was doing at work and tried his best to find out how Gary was handling his money. Gary counted on their interventions. It did not feel like he was really on his own, and he knew they were there to fall back on. His leaving was a pretense. Their dysfunctional roles stayed the same.

5. *The unaccepted leaving.* In this case the parents do not accept their adult child's leaving home. They disregard the adult status or separate life, responding as if there were no change. They make it clear from the time of departure that the leaving is unacceptable to them.

In his novel *Godric,* Frederick Buechner tells about the life of a twelfth-century English holy man, Godric of Finchale. In the chapter entitled "How Godric Left Home" we see how his departing day was unacceptable to his parents.

"Farewell, Father. Mother, farewell," I said. Aedwen [his mother] took and slowly turned my face from side to side as if to rummage it for something there she'd lost or feared to lose. She gave me a sack of berries and a wool cap. She wept no tears, and not a word came from her lips.

Aedlward, my father, was sitting by the fire. He did not rise. He only raised one hand, then spoke the only word of all the words he ever spoke to me that I remember still as his.

"You'll have your way, Godric," he said, and to this day that word he spoke and that raised hand are stitched together in my mind.

I believe my way went from that hand as a path goes from a door, and though many a mile that way has led me since, with many a turn and crossroad in between, if ever I should trace it back, it's to my father's hand that it would lead. I kissed him on his head then, for he'd turned away to watch the flames. He smelled of oxen and of rain. It was the last I ever saw of him. (Buechner 1980:23)

When a man leaves home, some scrap of his heart waits there against his coming back. . . . He [Godric] carried in his heart an empty place that only those he'd left behind could fill, and to that end alone he journeyed . . . to find that scrap. (Buechner 1980:50)

6. *Matter-of-fact leaving.* In this leaving there is a simple announcement and a clear acceptance of the new arrangement. Mixed feelings are openly acknowledged and dealt with. This intentional choice implies that adult children have developed enough sense of self to know what they want and determine to be on their own.

Kelsey had been planning to move into an apartment for more than a year. When she and her girlfriend finally saved enough money to furnish, decorate and manage the first month's rent, Kelsey's parents were pleased to help with the move and to celebrate her leaving with their best wishes.

The Fight for Separation

Have you ever noticed how often children and parents who are about to be separated engage in a fight prior to the separation? It is almost as if it is the only way for the child to leave. The parents are then more willing to let the child go, and the child is more able to leave, realizing life at home is not always a bed of roses.

A friend was recalling this to me (Boni). Her son was leaving for college, and she was sharing how frustrating the summer had been. She and her husband had rarely had difficulty with their son while he was in high school, yet now that he was preparing to leave in a few months, every discussion seemed to end in an argument. When the time came for him to leave, everyone was eager. He had become too disruptive to the rest of the family. Now she was counting the days! The whole family was ready, not out of a sense of hope for him and his future, but out of exhaustion with him and their relationship. While their family had seemed to be a close one, true feelings were rarely expressed. Since talking about how they felt did not seem to be an option, perhaps this was the only way he felt he could leave.

In this case this family missed an opportunity. How much better it would have been if the parents and their son could have talked about what was going on inside each of them. Of course he was fearful of what was ahead, yet he wanted to go anyway. Of course they would miss him a lot, but they also wanted him to succeed. But what was communicated was an inability to resolve their relationship. What he felt was their need to hold him back. He ended that turmoil by being so difficult they finally let him go, with hard feelings for everyone.

Maggie had been estranged from her mother for several years. After high school she got a job and continued to live at home for two years before moving out. She remembered those years as being very difficult for everyone. Her mother continued to enforce a curfew, inspect her room regularly and read her mail. Maggie was an obedient daughter and tried hard to live by her mother's rules. But she had dreams of getting her own apartment and establishing a life apart from her mother. A single parent, her mother had become dependent on her daughter in ways she did not realize. And the thought of her daughter's leaving her was an intolerable one.

Eventually Maggie pleaded with her mother to allow her to move into an apartment with a friend, but her mother held her ground, insisting that Maggie continue to live at home. Before long Maggie began breaking her curfew, keeping her room as untidy as she wanted and ranting about her mother's reading her mail. Conflict became a daily event until in a rage her mother kicked her out of the house. When Maggie came for therapy, they had not spoken since her leaving—a huge loss to both of them.

Some form of emotional separation will happen during the leaving-home time. If we do not give our children permission to leave, to explore life with our blessing, most children will leave without our blessing. They may leave with angry words and a force that may shock us. They may do so with tears and turmoil. Or they may withdraw from us emotionally and effect a leaving that way. The loss is not only theirs but ours as well. We miss out on blessing them with our love and assurance of hope for them, as well as the blessing of ongoing relationships with adult children.

Celebration

Our children's leaving home needs to be a time ultimately of celebration. It is acceptable to rejoice when our children progress through life stages in a healthy way. After my (Boni's) son, Aaron, left for college, a friend asked, "Aren't you proud?" I realized I was. In spite of the pain of his leaving, I was a very proud mother, for this separation said many things about him and about us as a family.

As Aaron's parents, we knew that his decision to leave was well thought out and his plans made with great effort. He had a goal and was already working toward achieving that goal. And he was taking risks, something we knew did not come easily for him.

We too had made adjustments that were significant. We were capable of letting him go, even if it hurt. We were willing to put aside the feelings of the moment and to look toward the good of this son we loved. We had the capacity to love and to let go when that was what was called for. It hurt, but it also felt good. And a part of me wanted to celebrate the capacity each of us had to participate in this leaving in this way.

So we prayed with our son, for his future and again for God's direction in his life. We did our best to let him know he was going with our blessing and with the blessing of his God. It was a wish for his success and a belief in God's protection. It was a way of confirming his separation while affirming his continued connectedness.

God's Child

What causes the leave taking to be so difficult for so many of us? Sometimes it is a lack of trust in God that creates our tight hold on our children. We act out the belief that we can keep them safe or that life with us in charge will be better for them than the life God has for them. Our theology tells us differently, but our behaviors demonstrate a lack of trust in God's care for our children.

We know that God has protected our children through their youth and that by God's mercy they have reached adulthood. Any parent who sees a child swinging from trees and climbing too high at the playground knows there is no way we can keep him or her from hurt. We do the best we can and we trust our child to our Lord for safety. Our children go through their school days meeting heretical philosophies in the media, on television and with their friends. We pray for God's keeping of their minds, their souls and their bodies. And we do our best to instruct them in the way of the cross and hope it sticks. But when they are out of eyesight, the stakes seem higher, the temptations greater, and we worry about whether we have done enough. How will they ever stay safe without us?

Last fall Boni's daughter Karlie decided she needed to do something rather than study. She decided to take a semester off from college and go to Africa to work in a mission for three months. Of course we asked all the usual questions one might ask in that situation. "Why Africa? Do you know how much disease is there? Do you know how unsafe those countries are? Do you know anything about this place?" We were worried for her but also immensely thankful for her courage and her desire to serve. For three months she was in the bush, working sixteen hours a day with children, under a mission we knew nothing about. We could not call her on the phone, and her letters arrived weeks after she had written them. When they did arrive they were not always comforting. In one letter she would talk of seeing the greatest amount of disease and poverty that she could imagine, and in the next letter she would talk of bungee jumping. Only one thing was certain. God knew where she was, and she was in his care.

I am so grateful that God gave us the courage to support Karlie in this desire. What a life-changing experience it was for her, and how awful it would have been for us to attempt to limit her vision. As we went through the weeks of not knowing where she was we prayed. We learned to turn worry into prayer. We attempted to discipline our minds away from worry, but when anxious thoughts came we committed them to God. After all, he was the only one with any power in the situation. What could our worry do? The decision was to pray and to trust the Lord of the universe with the care of our daughter.

There is so much to take to the Lord. Pray for the new independence young adults are seeking. Pray for their roommates, their professors, their employers and their friends. Pray for their new church, their spiritual growth and that they find a place to serve. Pray that they remember their roots and that they find their wings. What else is there to do? Can we bind them to us with an everlasting umbilical cord? Can we watch over them forever? Can we prepare the way for them as we did when they were young, keeping them forever dependent and prohibiting their growth? Of course not. The training has been done; the time has come. We must graciously let them go.

Turning worry into prayer is a lifelong learning task. Most of us have had to learn to do this in many areas of life, not just with our children. Yet Jesus clearly teaches us to trust our heavenly Father for what we need. Our task is to "strive first for the kingdom of God and his righteousness" (Mt 6:33). As we do that, God will provide what he believes we need.

The Goal Is Interdependence

Our hope is that our children will be responsible citizens, taking their place in the kingdom of God, capable of having meaningful relationships and able to care for themselves and their children. It seems like a lot when you consider that for many children life was so different before the age of eighteen. Parents were responsible for them and their decisions and sometimes even their faith. They were cared for and directed (or controlled), and sometimes they took little responsibility for their lives. Then suddenly—freedom! And with the longed-for freedom comes a responsibility they often do not know what to do with.

A dependent is one who is subordinate; one who relies on another to care for and direct him or her. Independence then is the capacity to do those things for oneself. Independent persons think and act on their own behalf. Independence works best when it is a gradual process of letting go in which the children work themselves into the job of responsible adult. As we will see in the next chapter, helping a child separate (and thus be independent) is best done beginning when the child is young. Yet the period of leaving is crucial to the goal we hope to accomplish. Each family will do it a little differently, and many styles are healthy. We will see more of this in chapter three. The important point is to work together on it, to acknowledge what is happening and to launch our children into a life that feels somewhat stable for them.

Then the ultimate goal of interdependence becomes possible. When our adult children have separated properly, they can form relationships with us and others with a capacity for healthy connections. Interdependence is the capacity for mutual relationships. They are neither dependent nor independent but mutually interdependent with significant family members. Interdependence is the model Christ gives his church and we hope to pass on to our children. If we have done our job well, they will come to depend on God to work in and through them as they develop relationships and carve out their future. Knowing they are responsible to God for their choices and the consequences of their decisions, we can acknowledge our human limitations as parents, knowing we have done our best to rear them. Now we let them go, to rely on their heavenly parent for the rest of their lives.

As we live interdependently with our children, we can take great joy in the mutual relationship that develops. Helping to move our children from dependence through independence and on into an interdependent life is our task as the parents of young adults.

Exercise
Take a fifteen- to twenty-minute quiet time and reflect on the day you left home. Let yourself visualize the scene, who was there and what emotions or words were being expressed. Now take a minute to draw the scene on a piece of paper. Do not get hung up on what the picture looks like (stick figures are fine), but draw as many of the emotional reactions as possible. Take a moment to ponder your picture. What do you see that you never saw before? What helps you understand what your own teenagers may be feeling? Share your picture with a trusted friend or your own family and describe to them your own leaving-day experience.

2

Coming of Age

....

T he age of majority is recognized in all cultures as a time when persons are held accountable for their behavior. It marks the day the child becomes an adult. In the Jewish tradition the bar mitzvah or bat mitzvah is an example of how the family and community celebrate this special day in the life of a young adult. At thirteen years of age the young person has the awesome task of standing in front of family, friends and the entire faith community to read the Torah. The child has worked hard to learn Hebrew for this crowning moment. When the reading is finished, the rabbi pronounces, "Now he is a man" or "Now she is a woman." Even though some in the audience may not see the person as adult and may perhaps snicker at the pronouncement, this is the day that adult status is acknowledged. The ceremony, followed by a wonderful feast of specially prepared foods, music and dancing, celebrates publicly this change.

In all cultures children and families progress through developmental stages toward this end. Understanding these individual stages as well as the stages of family life can help us make this transition with grace and harmony. Certain conditions in the makeup of the family will have an impact on every individual in that family: the number of children in the family, the age span of the siblings, the special needs of any member, different life stages represented (age span between children in same family) and the individual development of each member. Other life circumstances that influence the leaving-home experience include financial considerations: whether one lives in a single, dual or blended family household and the involvement of extended family members. Still there are fairly predictable tasks to be accomplished by each member throughout the developmental life process. Whereas there is variability along the way and an ebb and flow within and between stages, it is helpful to gauge a person's development as he or she progresses from dependency in the early years to relative independence in later years.

In the Beginning
Let's start at the beginning of the developmental process. Attachment and bonding are key events in the first few years of life. Parents are expected to meet the needs of their young children by being faithful and reliable when they respond to their dependent children. Children rely exclusively on their primary caretaker(s) for physical affection, protection and caring for their emotional needs. In fact the child's central source of security comes through emotional connection with the parents. This lays the foundational groundwork for a child's capacity to eventually develop a sense of trust.

In the earliest months children cannot distinguish their self from that of their significant caretaker(s). They are one and the same in that there is no sense of where the child's skin leaves off and the parent's skin begins. Whether infants are carried next to their parent's body in a carrier or put in a crib beside the bed, they experience nurture and comfort from those who have the power to care for their needs. When their stomachs are satisfied and they feel comfortable and warm through loving touch and protection, they can develop a sense of trust and security about the world in which they live. When basic needs are not met, that deprivation leads to belief in a world that is threatening and untrustworthy.

As children grow they are continually challenged by tasks such as walking, talking and toilet training that gradually move them to independence. Little Jenny has just begun to crawl, giving her the newfound freedom to move away from her mother or father. Note how much pleasure she gets from crawling far away from them but also how she turns around to make sure they are not too far out of sight. She crawls back likety-split when she becomes scared or insecure, because she has gone too far away. Or she sits crying, waiting for her parents to rescue her. Even though she knows how to crawl back, she feels dependent on her parents' help and needs to know they recognize her limitations.

All along the developmental path children oscillate between dependence and independence when they are learning to master a particular task. Not long after Jenny has learned to crawl with verve and confidence, walking becomes the next challenge. Taking her first, unsteady step is a pretty frightening feat. She tries and tries again as she is coaxed by her parents, and soon she toddles from one piece of furniture to the next with increased confidence and pride. Still a little shaky, she takes a hard fall and decides to go back to crawling for a while. But, having gained a taste for walking, she gets up the courage to try again. Note that she doesn't give up crawling right away but fluctuates from the old to the new behavior until she finally masters walking. Once in a while she goes back to crawling as a preferred mode, but at some point she gets beyond crawling and makes walking her preference. Then she discovers more advanced possibilities when she learns to run, jump and skip.

Gradually the child gains more capacity for independence. Danny, age seven, was thrilled with his new possibilities of being independent from his parents until he strayed too far from them at the county fair. When he looked around he realized he was lost, and that is when he lost his cool. Fear took over when he realized he would never be able to find them in the crowd. Being separated before you are ready to be on your own is intolerable.

This is the kind of anxiety children feel when they are left to fend for themselves before they are ready. Parents who fail to guide and direct their children through these young ages leave them vulnerable and ineffective. Panic strikes when you are too young to be on your own but independence is forced upon you. Giving room for fluctuation between dependency and independence is the most important lesson for parents to learn. When our children know they can depend on us as they learn to be independent, they will find the stability they need to eventually make a smooth separation during late adolescence.

Adolescents grow gradually into adulthood. It is normal for teenagers to resort to childish ways one moment and leap into sophistication beyond their years the next. There is a great deal of ambivalence during this stage for parents as well as teens. A cartoon depicts this thought. A teenager is lying on her bed talking into a tape recorder, and the caption says, "Parents are so stupid! Don't they know that all I want them to do is to take care of me and leave me alone?" This seems to sum it up nicely. How do we both take care of them and leave them alone? It is a tricky business to balance the giving and taking, the holding on and letting go.

I (Judy) remember asking myself, "Where did my little girl go?" when my thirteen-year-old daughter and I went shopping for a winter coat. She selected a long, elegant, fur-trimmed coat from one clothes rack while I came up with a cute, red, embroidered one from another part of the store. Obviously there was a clash about how grown up she was. I quietly put the coat I had picked back on the rack and applauded her for finding such a beautiful coat. I needed to give up my need to keep her young and support her desire to be more grown up on that day.

Just three years later, shortly after Jacque had gotten her driver's license, I remember cautioning her to be careful driving because of the rainy weather. She looked at me with some disdain and spoke in a rather indignant tone of voice, "Oh, Mom! I can handle it just fine!" Ten minutes later I got a phone call from a frightened little girl saying, "Mommmy, I got in a little accident! Can you come? I need you!" This time I was there to support her when she needed to depend on me. So back and forth they go, and back and forth we go, as we both prepare for that leave-taking day.

On the Way to Adulthood

The three major tasks of young adulthood are developing autonomy, developing interpersonal relationships and developing purpose. It may be helpful to think about these three categories as you try to gauge your son's or daughter's readiness for leaving. We will consider the subtasks under each major task to help you determine how your adolescent is doing.

Developing autonomy includes establishing emotional, financial, and structural independence. It doesn't mean that your teenager is completely independent but that he or she is moving in that direction.

Being able to establish and maintain the personal support of peers and adults outside the family is a good indicator that a person has achieved a sufficient level of emotional maturity. Bonding with significant others who encourage, affirm, challenge and confront shows that the family is no longer the single source of emotional exchange.

In terms of finances (we will discuss this in more detail in later chapters), it means that your teenagers are able to get and keep a job and to pay out of their own pocket for the special things they want. Even though parents may provide most of the basics (housing, food, education) they will find ways to contribute toward that goal.

Many students find part-time jobs to help meet their college expenses. This gives them the freedom to meet expenses when they need personal items or want to go to social events. Summer jobs can be a means of helping with tuition or housing expenses. Many students do not have help from their families for college and are completely in charge of their college expenses. Structural autonomy indicates an ability to care for and maintain personal interests such as paying for car insurance and gas, being responsible for laundering clothes, cooking, arranging for transportation needs, making dental and doctor appointments as needed, and so on. In all these accomplishments they are demonstrating the ability to take responsibility for their lives.

Developing interpersonal relationships includes establishing and becoming emotionally intimate with same- and opposite-sex friends as well as learning tolerance for those of different race, ethnicity, age, religion, economic or political persuasion. Horizons are expanded as our teenagers are exposed to many different ways of being. They will grow through developing an ongoing awareness and appreciation for different approaches to life as they learn to tolerate the belief systems and behavior of others. It will be a time when personal and family belief structures get challenged.

Through dialogue and encounters with others, one's personal beliefs take shape and are more clearly defined. If our teenagers have open minds, embrace new ideas as well as delineate their own ideas and values, they can achieve a newfound clarity in their relationships. Communication and conflict resolution skills are developed through these important interpersonal interactions. Establishing oneself as a sexual being, dating, making decisions about emotional and physical closeness with dating partners are important aspects of becoming adult. It is a time to know and be known in more intimate and personal ways.

Last is *developing purpose.* This task includes making work, career and lifestyle choices and establishing a moral and spiritual value system that is congruent with one's personal beliefs. This can be a testy time between parents and their children, for teenagers often question parental values and beliefs in order to clarify and establish their own sense of right and wrong. Parents may be tempted to use their influence and power ("we won't give you money to go to that college") when it comes to this area of development rather than let their children grapple with the doubts and questions they have. It can be an anxious time, causing parents to hold on even harder, especially when you believe your children are heading in a direction that meets with your disapproval or seems to lead to disaster.

The main thing to remember about this task is that it takes time for young adults to find their way and establish values and beliefs that they can live by and claim as their own. When you see congruence in what they say and what they do, you know their values and choices are becoming a deep part of who they choose to be. Patience is needed while they are finding their way. When you can answer questions honestly rather than defensively and give good reasons for your faith and moral value system, you will help them through the process. Allowing them to try out their ideas on you and asking them good questions so they can discover where their beliefs are taking them can be a wonderfully enriching experience for parents and young adults.

I remember when Joel came home from college and began expressing political views that were quite different from those we (Judy and her husband, Jack) held. At first we found ourselves a little hurt that he had not swallowed our ideas hook, line and sinker. Jack started to challenge him in an aggressive way, which only made Joel hold tighter to his ideas. Even though Jack could easily shoot holes in Joel's half-thought-out positions, it was the way to assure he would find ammunition to challenge back. Fortunately we realized what we were doing and took a different tack.

The next time Joel tried out his new thoughts on us, we showed interest in how he was coming to his conclusions. Instead of being critical, we helped him think more deeply about the opinions that accompanied this point of view. We were not trying to persuade him but to help him understand how and why he was thinking the way he was. It was helpful to remind ourselves that when we were in college, we held to many of the same views he was espousing. It was not that they were wrong; we were at a different place in our beliefs at this point in life. Joel needed our respect. We needed to show tolerance for his views that were different from our own. This approach gave him the freedom to ask us questions and to learn more about our ideas as well. He still doesn't have all his ideas in concrete, but his process of developing purpose and of forming his personal values and beliefs is becoming a congruent part of his life. We are proud of our son, a young man of character and integrity.

It Is Different for Daughters

Standard assumptions about female development have been questioned in recent years. It is clear that there are different developmental pressures in childhood for males and females. For example, parents tend to give sons more freedom as well as put more expectations on them to achieve. In *The Reproduction of Mothering* (1978) Nancy Chodorow shows how psychological identification of the female infant with her mother generates more capacity for empathy, attachment and interpersonal sensitivity in gender-role formation. The male child, however, needs to separate from his mother at an earlier age in order to identify with his same-gender parent. He often does this by rejecting feminine qualities like nurture and attachment so he can prove his maleness to others. Therefore, when it is time for leaving home, he has a head start when it comes to self-identity and separation. He may have an easier time leaving home because of this early break from his mother. Since girls have not had to separate from their mothers to find their female identity, they have a head start when it comes to connection and intimacy. For this reason it may be more difficult for them to leave home, since they have been rewarded for staying connected rather than for being separate and independent.

The point we are making is that girls and boys develop differently due to these family relationships and experiences. The power of socialization cannot be overlooked. If our daughters are taught to value family connection, they will be more hesitant to leave home, especially if leaving creates disharmony in the home. They are usually urged to play the role of peacemaker, nurturer and caretaker, making it more difficult to establish good boundaries between themselves and their families. Defining happiness in terms of marriage and having children may cause a daughter agony when she chooses to focus on a career. Expectations that devotion to the needs of others should be her highest priority may cause self-incriminating judgments. She may feel guilty or label herself as selfish when she takes independent action. Being socialized to be other-directed, she can easily be criticized for autonomous decisions and choices. Viewing her as the weaker sex, her parents may be more protective and hold on more tightly to her than they would with a son. If she does something exceptionally well she may be criticized for being aggressive or overly ambitious.

For all these reasons it can be more difficult for a young woman to separate from her family than it is for a young man. She may hesitate to leave home on a future adventure because she needs to please her parents or take care of their needs rather than think of her own desires. Perhaps this explains why more girls than boys report homesickness when they go to college. A time of feeling groundless (without family connectedness) may be more difficult for young women.

A Sufficient Self

Whether one is male or female, leaving home and saying goodby in a good way takes a sufficient amount of differentiation. This key concept of Murray Bowen (1978), a family therapist, helps us gauge the readiness of an adult child to make a healthy leaving. *Differentiation* is a term used to describe an individual who has a solid sense of self that comes from an ability to know one's thoughts and feelings. In addition that person is able to take responsible action for him- or herself rather than reacting to what others say or want. Having an adequate basis for action demands that one be able to refrain from emotional reactivity and make choices and accept the consequences of those actions.

A person who has a sufficient self can negotiate leaving home without having to cut off prematurely or remain overly attached after he or she leaves. Being able to function optimally around significant others without feeling overly responsible, controlled or impaired by them indicates a strong level of differentiation. In contrast, extreme dependence on or isolation from others indicates a low level of differentiation. In Western cultures independence is often overrated, whereas in Eastern cultures dependency is generally overrated. At the heart of differentiation is interdependency, the capacity to affirm self and others. The young person who has a solid sense of self is the one who has the deepest capacity to make significant connections with others. In light of constantly changing relationships, it takes endless courage and effort to create a healthy balance between the two. Learning to be a self, capable of independence and interconnectedness, is a lifelong process.

The dramatic end of childhood dependence is the beginning of a personal search for an independence and interdependence. It is a time when young people are trying to find their own voices in the midst of many competitive voices from parents and society trying to tell them who they are. Finding that self as a youth is often a time of inner confusion and turmoil. Frederick Buechner writes of his own experience in *The Sacred Journey.*

> We search, on our journeys, for a self to be, for other selves to love, and for work to do. . . . I can remember at least the sense of having become, or started to become, a self with boundaries somewhat wider than and different from those set me by my family. I no more knew who I was then than in most ways I know who I am now, but I knew that I could survive more or less on my own in more or less the real world. I knew, as I had not before, the sound of my own voice both literally and figuratively—knew something of what was different about my way of speaking from anybody else's way and knew something of the power of words spoken from the truth of my own heart or from as close to that truth as I was able to come then. (Buechner 1982:72-73)

I (Boni) have noticed this development in my daughter Karlie. She has had a need to feel that clear sense of self, different from me or any other, since early adolescence. And often I have struggled against it, trying to make her an "us" before she had a firm "me." As she is about to graduate from college, it came up again as I found myself pushing against her postcollege plans. Karlie plans to work in a Third World country, most likely Thailand or Zaire. Her heart is in Africa. My heart is in her safety, and Zaire is not a safe country to live or work in now. Recently I have been able to make clearer attempts to relinquish my desire for her and to affirm her sense of self. I told her what I believed about her. She is a bright young woman. She is a Christian directed by God. And she has the capacity to make this decision without me. Her sense of self is clear enough that she would have gone where she believed she should go, with or without my support. But it felt good to affirm her ability to make good decisions and to know what is right for her. That affirmation solidifies her as a separate person and helps me let her go.

Launching Losses

Regardless of how easy or difficult it is for our male and female children to leave or how differentiated they are, loss is a significant part of the launching. Whether or not we recognize this fact, the emotional and physical bonds change and things will never be quite the same. Family members must reorganize themselves to make up for the missing member. The family balance shifts to accommodate for the gaps by establishing new roles and renegotiating family relationships. The changes reverberate throughout the family, and unless the family attends to the loss, members are likely to feel fragmented, isolated and out of sorts with one another.

Siblings in particular are affected by the restructuring in the family. Just as leaving home can be an ordeal between parents and their adult children, it is also an ordeal for brothers and sisters. It can be painful for the sibling(s) left behind. Whether the leave taking is viewed as a celebration or a rejection, it always disrupts the status quo of the sibling relationships. Unattended conflicted relationships may be a source of guilt, or guilt may come from extra privileges and achieving a new place of importance after the older brother or sister is gone.

In other situations the leaving of older siblings gives younger children an opportunity to establish a different relationship with their parents. They finally get the attention of their parents, unshared by older siblings.

This seemed true of Sarah, the youngest of the Piper children. Although she loved her older brother and sister deeply, she often had to work hard to get in her ideas and topics of discussion at the dinner table. She had a lifetime of sharing her parents' attention at sports events and other activities she participated in. When her second-older sibling left home, she finally had center stage and seemed to delight in it. Now both parents attended her basketball games, not needing to divide time among multiple sports events. Dinner conversation seemed to center on her interests, and eventually she even got the bigger bedroom. Though she missed her brother and sister deeply, she enjoyed the special attention this period of life brought her.

In other cases it becomes an additional burden, as well as an advantage for a sibling, after an older brother or sister leaves. Catherine, the baby of the family, had many advantages after her older siblings left. She now had a beautifully decorated bedroom and a television all to herself. Yet she felt incredibly lonely and lost without her sibling cohorts. The freedom and availability of her parents did not make up for the missed company. While her parents could now attend all her school events, she didn't anticipate how much she would miss having her brother or sister there to cheer her on. While she could invite friends over without having to worry about anyone else competing for the space, it was a less exciting place without the presence of her siblings. She and her parents went out to eat more often at nice restaurants, but she was also the single focus of attention when things went wrong. There was no one to bounce off her ideas or negative feelings when her parents seemed unreasonable. Since dinnertime had always been packed with talk, laughter and differences of opinions, she now felt strange about the quiet at that same table. She also had to pick up the slack by doing additional chores and felt more responsible for intervening between her parents when they argued. Feeling the edge to her parents' relationship, she desperately wanted to share with her siblings.

Sibling birth order can also be a troublesome factor in leaving-home experiences. When my (Judy's) older sister got married after she finished high school and moved across country to join her husband, who was enlisted in the navy, I was given opportunities to achieve in ways that had not been apparent to me before. I took full advantage and made plans to go to college. Later I felt guilty that my sister's choice to marry and have children at an early age made it possible for me to receive additional financial support from my parents. A middle child who sometimes played second fiddle, I had been promoted to the privileged first chair in the orchestra. The fact that I gained after my sister left was something I had to reconcile with her later in life. I also had to deal with my frustration of being cheated out of my younger brother's basketball success the year after I left home. We had been close friends all through high school, and it was a great loss for me when I was not able to attend his final state championship game.

Sibling gains and losses in the leaving-home process are poignantly described by Buechner. He tells how Godric's brother wept when he left, perhaps feeling the loss of the male connection or having the added responsibility of caring for his aging parents. However, it was Godric's sister, Burcwen, who had the most difficulty with his leaving. When Godric went to say goodby to her, this is what transpired.

"I'm going with thee, Godric," she said. Then she threatened to hang herself with a rope she took from her basket unless he would let her come along with him. Godric responded, "But for now, your life is here and my life's mine to find and fashion where I may. So Godric goes and Burcwen stays." He said this with all the firmness he could muster so Burcwen would not run after him. After taking a few steps he turned around to see that she had climbed up a tree and was threatening to hang herself.

I saw she laughed, and laughter too was part of what was choking me, but there was madness in our mirth, for I was daring her to die and Burcwen daring me to drive her to. So then I ran to save her while I still had time. I plucked her off her branch like a treed cat, and we scuffled, laughing in the rain, while I trussed her underneath the arms and hoisted her until she hung there dangling from her tree again. When she saw there was nothing she could do, she went so grave and still she could have been an angel overhead. (Buechner 1980:25-27)

Burcwen, finally resigned to staying home, gave Godric a parting gift. It was a cross she had whittled from two pieces of wood and bound with a few strands of her own hair. Godric hung it around his neck as they said their final goodby. Later in his life Godric remembered that leaving-home day and pondered the meaning of leaving his beloved sister behind.

I've wondered since if maybe why she brought that rope was not to hang herself but so I'd have the means to make her stay. I think that in some corner of her heart she wanted to be bound against her own wild will to go with me as in the wilds of me I yearned to cut her down so she could come. But off I went and never gave another backward glance lest like Lot's wife I'd turn into a pillar of salt as my own tears. (Buechner 1980:27)

There is sadness in saying goodby to those you love and leave behind. There is pain in leaving as there is pain in staying behind. Let's acknowledge the loss by finding a time and place to express what we feel so we can make peace with ourselves and the one who leaves.

A Ritual of Leaving

Just as Burcwen gave Godric a parting gift when he left home, such gift-giving rituals can help with the disparate feelings of joy and loss when a family member leaves home. Graduation day, for example, is an important event that signifies a rite of passage into adulthood. This is the day we set aside for everybody to celebrate and acknowledge that event. Private family leaving-home rituals can provide a similar opportunity to say goodby. The purpose is to mark this event in a meaningful way.

In planning such an experience each family member is asked to do something special that gives meaning to the launching of the particular member. Perhaps a letter, a picture or a symbol can be given as a way to express what that person means to you and what you will miss about him or her. The one who is leaving can do a similar thing. It is a simple ceremony that invites members to exchange thoughts and feelings in the family context. It can include a burial of past hurts or disappointments so that each member can wipe the slate clean and embrace a future unencumbered by unfinished business. Here is an example of how the Pederson family made use of a goodby ritual when Tim left home.

Tim and his family had been at odds for about two years before he finally left home to take a job in another state. Everyone was relieved when Tim announced his plans to leave home. Their family therapist wanted to help them say a good goodby, so she asked each family member to bring an object to the final therapy session to mark this transition in the life of the family.

There was a sense of anticipation when they gathered for the final session. Mr. Pederson started things off by pulling out his old pocket-knife. He and Tim had used this knife many times during their Boy Scout father-and-son campouts. Although the past years had been a struggle, Mr. Pederson wanted Tim to remember the many good times they had together as father and son. Mrs. Pederson brought a letter she had written for the occasion. She read out loud her words about freedom and forgiveness. Admitting her resentful feelings about a particular incident that had occurred, she asked forgiveness for her judgmental attitude. Tim was able to receive her apology, and a burden lifted between them.

His sister gave Tim a trinket mouse he had won for her at a county fair some years earlier. She told him how much it meant to her to have a big brother who had protected her when she felt as small as that mouse. Tim's younger brother had drawn a picture of the two of them riding bikes together with a note saying how much he would miss Tim.

Then it was Tim's turn. Everyone was eager to know what he had brought. With a grin on his face, he brought out the key to his bedroom door. He had used this key to keep others out, but now that he had a place of his own he hoped the family would use the room with good thoughts about him.

This exercise helped the family remember some good times and acknowledge some difficult times. Along with a few tears, a few smiles and expressions of goodwill, the family was able to say a good goodby.

You can see how each member participated in a unique way. The thoughtful preparation that went into the selection of each symbol provided a way to say something important. The son could now leave with the family's blessing, and the family could reintegrate into home life without him. The emotional connection remains intact after the physical separation occurs.

A spiritual dimension adds richness to the ritual. Belief that God is at work in the life of the leaving-home member helps us let go. We can surround that one with our prayers of God's blessing. We can covenant to be faithful prayer warriors. We remain emotionally connected through our prayers. While the empty bedroom will be a reminder of the loss, it can also be an impetus to offer a prayer. When we lie in our beds waiting to hear familiar footsteps coming up the stairs, we can ask for God's presence with our son or daughter. When the absence leaves a silent sting that is too sharp to bear, we can write a letter, send a care package or make an encouraging phone call. We can let them go with our blessing and with God's blessing.

Developing as God's Child

Each of us is in the process of becoming the person God wants us to be. Paul writes in the second letter to the church at Corinth that "all of us, with unveiled faces, seeing the glory of the Lord as though reflected in a mirror, are being transformed into the same image from one degree of glory to another; for this comes from the Lord, the Spirit" (2 Cor 3:18). Development is a natural part of being human for the Christian. In profound ways our young adult children are developing physically, emotionally and spiritually. If they were not making changes and growing, we would be concerned.

In truth, we all keep changing. Molding ourselves into the image of Christ is a lifelong work of the Holy Spirit in us. Our tasks are not always as clearly spelled out as those of a young adult, but nonetheless we are called to move developmentally along with our children.

For many parents the task is to live again as husband and wife without children. For others shifts in the family through a child's leaving will bring new and different challenges. Whatever pain and change this leaving-home stage brings your way, it brings a corresponding opportunity for you and your family to grow in new directions.

Praise God for his grace to us as he proclaims to his children through Jeremiah, "For surely I know the plans I have for you, says the LORD, plans for your welfare and not for harm, to give you a future with hope" (Jer 29:11).

Exercise

What were some of the unique developmental phases of your son's or daughter's growing-up cycle? What specific gender messages were given in your home that had an impact on your child's leaving-home event? Take a moment to map out his or her cycle with the ups and downs your child has gone through. Consider how you can encourage your child at this point in the cycle.

3

Connection &
Separation Themes

••••••••••••••••••••••••

My *(Boni's) leaving-home day did not come until I was married.* I had gone to college in my hometown, so that was not a leaving for me. But after I married, my husband and I moved three thousand miles from my parents' home. We packed our car with all our possessions, said our tearful farewells and began the drive across the country. I remember looking back, seeing my parents standing in front of our home and feeling tremendous guilt. They approved of my marriage and had adjusted to our moving to Washington State, but I had an overwhelming feeling of betraying them as we began that drive off to the West.

My friend Paul talks of his leaving very differently. He planned to attend a community college that had no dorms available to students. One day during the summer after high-school graduation Paul came home to find his mother boxing up things in his room. After talking with her about what was going on, Paul realized that living at home was no longer an option—he had already overstayed his welcome. Paul had a feeling of guilt from a source different from mine. He quickly found a room to move into and began his independence earlier than he anticipated.

Carol's leaving came with great family conflict. When she was twenty, her parents forbade her to take a job promotion forty miles from home because it would require her moving out of their home. The whole family got involved in the battle. Her siblings were appalled that she would consider doing such a thing to Mom and Dad, her aunts and uncles came by to talk her out of the decision, and her parents stopped speaking to her. Taking the promotion was the most difficult decision of her life, she says, but one she has never regretted.

The Meaning of Leaving

The family system is greatly affected when a family member leaves. As we discussed in chapter two, the family will never be the same. But what accounts for the different effects leaving home has on a family? One explanation has to do with the amount of connection and adaptability in the family itself.

By *connection* we mean the value a family puts on unity and closeness and the stability that closeness provides for family members. It is a measure of the emotional bonding between family members. When being connected is a great priority in the family, this will influence the way the family responds to a member's leaving. Carol's family seemed to value connection highly. However, in Paul's family connection seemed less important.

Adaptability has to do with a family's ability to accept new concepts into the family and adjust to them. It is a measure of the family's ability to change and to be flexible. If a family is high on adaptability, this will affect their ability to cope during transitions. Carol's family would most likely be low on the adaptability scale and Paul's perhaps might rate higher.

Let's take a deeper look at the values and beliefs that are likely to influence families in relation to these two dimensions of family life. Then we will see how this impacts the leaving-home process.

David Olson, a family researcher, has designed a model to describe how families function along the two dimensions of connection and adaptability. The best way for you to understand these concepts is to get personally involved. We invite you to take a few minutes to pinpoint where you believe your family is on each of these dimensions.

First think of the definition of connection. How much emotional connection is there in your family? Mark a point on the continuum. Now do the same thing with the adaptability scale. Place an X on each continuum to indicate where you believe your family to be.

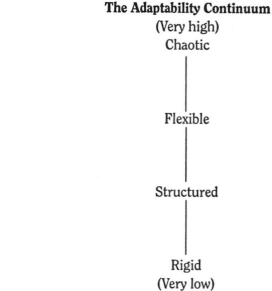

The Connection Continuum

(Very low)   (Very high)

Disengaged   Separated   Connected   Enmeshed

The Adaptability Continuum

(Very high)

Chaotic

|

Flexible

|

Structured

|

Rigid

(Very low)

Now place your family in one of the four quadrants of the model in the "circumplex model" in figure 1. This helps you identify the unique family values that go along with these family styles. Think specifically of how these preferences shape your response to the leaving-home stage of life.

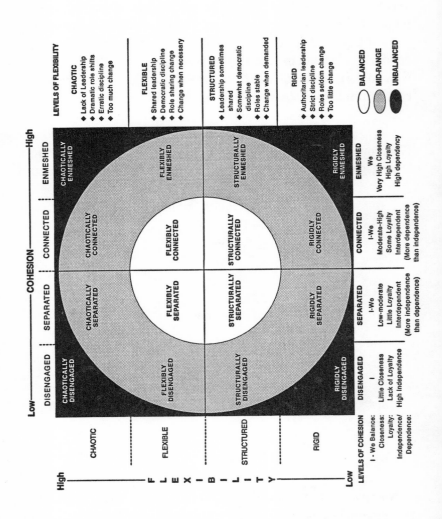

Figure 1.   Circumplex Model of Family Systems

Families Living on the Edge

The family types on the edge of the quadrant represent the particular imbalance in that family's behavior. Let's look at examples of each family in the extreme.

Members of *chaotically disengaged* families have little emotional connection or involvement with each other. These family members make separate and independent decisions about their lives. They spend little time together, lack parent-child closeness and have only small amounts of family loyalty. When it comes to discipline, the rules change frequently, and parental control is minimal. The parental leadership is erratic, and the roles often get confused for family members.

Jason describes his leaving home when he was sixteen. "I had to get out of that place," he confides. "My parents were glad to see me go because they felt I was just a troublemaker. They didn't seem to care if I was around and paid very little attention to me or my brothers and sisters. We all learned to fend for ourselves, so I figured I could make it on my own, cooking and managing my life in a hippie-type commune. That place was as laid-back and relaxed as my home, where everyone did their own thing. I was hoping for some close connections with my housemates, but no one was very good at nurturing each other. So we lived together, trying to find free love, but in reality I was lonely most of the time, just like I was in my family."

In *chaotically enmeshed* families, leadership by the parents is precarious in that no one clearly takes charge. There are frequent rule changes, and consequences for breaking rules are sporadic and inconsistent. Decisions are made impulsively, and negotiations seem endless. The one big difference from the chaotically disengaged family is the extreme emotional closeness and the overly dependent relationship between members. Decisions made by one member are subject to the wishes of the whole family. Family loyalty is a primary value, and no family member would think of doing anything to shame the family name, since this is viewed as an unpardonable act of disloyalty.

The Halbergs are an extremely close-knit family. No one seems to have friends outside the immediate and extended family. Spending a great deal of time together at home is the norm. There is an unspoken agreement to keep family secrets, so no one would think of exposing the eating disorder of the elder daughter. However, both parents are busy with the family business; they take little time to set up rules and discipline in the home. Geoffrey, the nineteen-year-old son, recently announced to the family that he had joined the army. His decision is in keeping with the family military history, but it was a decision made with no discussion with others in the family. His eldest sister, Hildegard (named after her grandmother), tries unsuccessfully to find a job but probably will end up working in her parents' flower business.

The *rigidly disengaged* family knows where the leadership lies. The parents are authoritarian, giving precise rules about how family members are to behave. There are strict consequences for disobedience to the rules and very little room for negotiation. There is an obvious lack of emotional involvement in these families, with minimal sharing of feelings or parent-child closeness. This family spends little time together, and each person looks to people outside the family for support and connection.

In the Nagato family each member keeps to himself or herself. There is little desire to spend time at home, where the atmosphere is tense and regimented. Lack of warmth and laughter make it impossible to enjoy family time together. Even though it is uncomfortable to be there, each family member is sure to be on time for the rigidly scheduled family meals. The punishment for disobeying any rule is too harsh a penalty to pay. Annette knew she wanted out of this strict environment as soon as possible, but she paid a high price for her independence. Being uninformed about sex, a topic too personal to discuss in her home, she got pregnant when she was twenty-three. Her partner, a man she hardly knew, was of a different race. Her parents proceeded to disown her, and she eventually had a hard future on her own as a single mother.

Rigidly enmeshed families have authoritarian leadership and highly controlling parents who enforce strict consequences of rule breaking. Yet there is a strong emphasis on family loyalty. Members are overly dependent on one another, and the good of the group has priority over the good of the individual. It's clear what the rules are and who enforces them. There are strictly defined roles for both males and females in the family.

Amanda and Daniel Brown, fraternal twins, are extremely close. Obedient children and loyal to their parents, they agreed to attend the same college their parents attended thirty years ago. Amanda signed up for a degree in home economics and Daniel for one in engineering.

After spending two years at the college, Daniel wanted to switch to the school of home economics to study family development. He, like his sister, had a great interest in understanding family dynamics. When Daniel broached the subject with their parents over the Christmas break, his choice was met with much disapproval. Mr. Brown belittled Daniel for wanting to go into a sissy field, and Mrs. Brown reacted with shock that Daniel was considering such a crazy idea when he knew how much his father wanted him to follow in his career footsteps. Amanda tried to support her brother, but to no avail. The family name was at stake. Daniel and Amanda returned to school defeated, knowing that it was out of the question to make independent choices. They had to pay too great a price in terms of their parents' disapproval.

A Middle Ground

As you can imagine, families in the extremes will have obvious difficulty as well as unique problems in getting through the leaving-home experience. The closer a family is toward the center, the more easily they will get through different family life stages because they are adaptable enough to change and have sufficient emotional connection to be stable. These families leave room for both a sufficient amount of closeness and adaptation.

Belonging and separation go together. When young people have a secure connection in the family and the family is flexible enough for each person to develop a unique core self, both the family and the individuals in it thrive. Those in more disengaged and chaotic homes leave without anyone paying much attention. Feeling isolated and disconnected, these persons search elsewhere for connection. That search may lead them into early marriage and/or pregnancy or to joining a community that promises love and stability. When there is too little connection or too little guidance, it is hard to achieve significant affiliation with others.

Families at the edge of the inner circles will experience leaving home as an ordeal. In fact many young people in the extremely enmeshed and/or rigid families may rebel in order to break out of these systems. Anger or loneliness spurs many of these young persons on. Often they will be disowned or will suffer shame unless they come back into the fold.

What About Cultural Differences?

The acceptable time to leave a family depends a great deal on the meaning given this event. Cultural and ethnic perspectives vary on when the proper leaving time is. For example, going through puberty rites at twelve, thirteen or fourteen establishes full adulthood in some cultures; arranged marriages or agreements may determine how and when a person leaves according to the norms of another culture. Western cultural norms are biased toward independence and separation, whereas other cultures value connection and belonging. In Korean families, for example, a son or a daughter is expected to live at home until he or she marries, no matter what the age. Extended family systems in these cultures give higher priority to interdependence and harmony than they do to separateness and chaos.

What specific factors have contributed to where you located your family on the model? What is your personal belief about successful leave taking? What are the constraints in your situation that may interfere with the leaving of your adult children? Are there some important cultural considerations that influence your views of connection and separation? What could you do to be more ready for the leaving to take place in a positive way?

Boundaries: Delicate Places of Proximity

All families need to establish appropriate boundaries between family members. Boundaries can either be too closed (no one has access to me) or too open (everyone has access to me). A boundary is defined as an imaginary line (imagine a line of dashes: - - -) that defines one's personal territory. It could be thought of as a border around an individual in the family or various family groups or subsystems (spousal, siblings, grandparents) within the family. It encompasses both physical space and emotional terrain, in that any particular family member decides when and who enters in or remains outside. Psychotherapists Nancy Wasserman Cocola and Arlene Modica Matthews explain the notion of boundary as a "delicate place of proximity. When people cross them carelessly, they are potential friction zones. When they are approached properly, as when citizens of one country may visit another country for a limited duration, there is little cause for border skirmishes" (Cocola and Matthews 1992, 74-75).

Parents and adult children need to establish boundaries between them that are appropriate and effective. This requires that family members clearly recognize the borders so we will not intrude into territory where we do not belong. When we are given an invitation to enter we can proceed, so that our interaction will be mutually beneficial. But we need to be careful to know the limits of what we as invited guests can do and say. By regarding the boundary as important we can help our adult children differentiate their thoughts and feelings from our thoughts and feelings. Respecting their wishes keeps skirmishes to a minimum.

Boundaries are the building blocks of living together in families because they help us be accountable to ourselves and those we live with. It is problematic for children to maneuver in unboundaried territory. It is scary to move toward the edge when you have no idea where the edge is. For some children the risk of falling is much too great, so they become overly dependent and less capable of self-determination. Other children reach too far in looking for a boundary that is not clearly drawn and in the process get way out of bounds. Finding themselves in situations they are not ready to handle, they experience tremendous anxiety and lack of confidence.

Parents provide the framework for appropriate boundary setting in the family. Defining personal and spousal/parental boundaries that cannot be intruded on or weakened by others sets a precedent. Having a clear definition about their role in the home, effective parents speak out of strength and authority. This models an environment in which children can develop good boundaries of their own by expressing what they believe, think and feel and by being aware of their intuitions, wants, needs and sensations. Having clear self-definition as well as honoring what other members think, feel, and want is a sign of well-boundaried parents. It means they can admit to inner feelings and work through core issues in their relationships with others. Well-defined parents have an uncanny ability to discern the real issues and dismiss the peripheral. Because the parents home in on the important issues, their children are able to respond readily to their requests. Through flexibility, fairness and firmness they have earned the right to be influential.

Finding the Right Balance
Families at the extremes tend to be unboundaried or overly boundaried. These parents are often taken advantage of, mistreated, feared, resisted or abused by their children. Inability to establish suitable boundaries usually has to do with an unawareness of self and weakness in the parental role. Overly developed boundaries become an impenetrable fortress, whereas insufficient boundaries indicate fragility and fusion. Either of these extremes can lead to neglectful, rigid, authoritarian or overly permissive parenting practices that result in underdevelopment for all concerned. A few examples will illustrate these unbalanced-boundary families.

Derek and his friend were having a friendly conversation in the family room. Derek's mother, Janet, walked into the room unannounced and immediately entered into the discussion with a strong opinion. Derek and his friend politely tolerated the intrusion, but it dampened their spirited discussion. They immediately remembered they had to meet some friends at the local pizza parlor. Derek excused himself to change into his jeans. Janet continued to dominate the conversation, telling the friend all about Derek's childhood. Suddenly she remembered a great picture of Derek as a nude baby, and she proceeded to knock on Derek's bedroom door to get the picture. Hearing her knock, Derek asked her to wait because he was dressing. Janet disregarded his request and barged into his room with the comment, "Oh, don't be silly! I'm just coming in to get your picture. I won't look at you anyway."

Need we say anything further? This mother not only violated the emotional and physical boundary of her son but also was unaware of the importance of respecting her son's territory. It's more than a skirmish. It is a battle that will probably keep Derek away from home as often as possible in the future.

Perhaps making boundaries seems easy, but it is a more difficult task than it sounds. Honoring physical boundaries may be a matter of allowing for closed doors, knocking before entering, not disturbing another's possessions, and the like. But boundaries that involve emotional comfort zones may be a bit more challenging and subtle. Think for a moment of how it feels to be in the presence of someone you care about and discover he or she has a different opinion on something that matters to you. Or think about how it feels to have one of your children express an attitude or a moral conviction that is different from yours. How do you respond when your daughter wears something you think looks awful or your son does something to his hair that you think looks weird?

Negotiating emotional boundaries is a task that takes wisdom, care and thought. If parents intrude carelessly they will undoubtedly be greeted with a barricade at the border crossing. When I attempt to determine how my adult children should dress, wear their hair or keep their room or whom they should associate with, work for or vote for, I demonstrate a lack of consideration for their thoughts, preferences, ideas and feelings. My behavior shows that I cannot tolerate differences between us. It says, "It is not okay to be you. You must be a form of me." This behavior would be characteristic of an enmeshed family whose message is "We must be alike."

Gathering the family together to talk through boundary problems can be a helpful way to bring understanding about this issue. In the case of boundary violations with Derek and his mother, Janet, a family meeting could have clarified the need for respecting boundaries by doing the following:

☐ Clarify how the personal boundary is being violated (insensitivity and interruption).

☐ Make sure everyone understands the reason for the boundary and why it is important to honor it (uninvited interaction and disregarded request).

☐ Discuss the impact of the boundary intrusion (relationship is strained).

☐ Brainstorm how the violator should make amends for breaking a boundary (apology and change of behavior).

☐ Set up and apply consequences for breaking a boundary (verbal reminder and continued accountability).

☐ Continually evaluate individual needs and interpersonal interaction (how are we doing on the agreement and our relationship after one month).

☐ Make necessary changes.

In contrast to the insufficient boundaries in Derek's home, the Lee family keep rigid boundaries that serve as barriers between family members. Such distinct personal boundaries give little room for involvement or interaction between members. Opinions, thoughts and feelings are clearly confined to each member's private world. There is no attempt to talk about issues and therefore little opportunity to clarify or have separate viewpoints challenged. Such rigid boundaries cheat this family out of a caring connection and fuller development of their ideas.

Min Lee grew up feeling alone with her thoughts and her emotions. She longed for someone to take interest in her. When she received a proposal for marriage from an inappropriate suitor, she tried to talk to her parents about him. Steve had never worked, drank a lot and had been verbally abusive in their relationship. Min's parents were not available for talking and did not seem to question anything about this new boyfriend. If they had any objections to him they never expressed those objections to her. Without parental guidance, she married Steve on an impulse. At least he seemed to want her around. What Min did not bargain for was how difficult it was to make an emotional connection with Steve after they were married. Her delusion that fusion equaled intimacy became a nightmare. She was as lonely as ever, and in addition faced a life of agony and abuse.

In these examples we see how both a lack of boundaries or overly rigid boundaries create problems in families. We need a healthy balance. When we can allow persons in, as well as keep them out when necessary, we demonstrate a capacity for genuine intimacy and self-determination.

Boundaries That Become You

Well-defined limits (boundaries) help each person in the family be aware of and sensitive to others. Limits give each member the ability to be powerful and creative in interactions. We can make healthy choices in relationships only when we know the possibilities as well as the restrictions. Having appropriate emotional boundaries means that we can express our inner desires as well as know the other person's reality. Boundaries keep us from resorting to fantasy or guessing games in our relationships. The integrity of each person is maintained by making sure boundaries are clarified, understood and respected. It helps us know how far we can go in a relationship when others let us know what they want and ask us what we want. Having boundaries validates ourselves as well as honors the needs and desires of others. Unless I am able to define who I am, it is difficult to keep appropriate boundaries. And it is through boundaries that we find self-definition.

The following statements reflect healthy boundaries. Read through the list and see how many statements are true of you.

☐ I usually know what I want and can ask others for what I want.

☐ I can make up my mind with reasonable ease.

☐ I can say no without difficulty.

☐ I have opinions about most things and people listen to them.

☐ People seldom take or use my things without asking me first.

☐ I know what I believe about most things.

☐ I listen to others without automatically accepting their opinions.

☐ I am sympathetic to others' feelings without making them my own.
☐ When I share personal matters with others, they keep confidences.
☐ I feel good about myself.
☐ I give about as much as I get in relationships.
☐ I determine to be accountable to God for my life.

If you are able to answer in the affirmative to the majority of these items, you most likely are keeping suitable boundaries in your personal relationships. If you waffle on most items, you are confused about and probably have difficulty making and keeping boundaries. If you answer no to most of these items, you may not understand what it means to establish appropriate boundaries in relationships.

Boundaries That Build Bridges

Parents who care about the emotional relationship with their children will learn how to establish firm yet flexible boundaries. Sometimes parents may choose to relax a boundary to fit the unique situation of a special child. (Since Bill has basketball practice this time of year, he will be able to eat dinner late.) Other times they remain firm. (We want everyone to be present for Sunday-night dinner because it's a special time together as a family.) Sometimes a weak boundary will be reinforced because it has indulged children in enabling ways. (Respecting our common living space means we must all take responsibility to clean up the kitchen after we eat.) Sometimes a boundary that seems right at one time is adjusted or changed at a later time. (We no longer need to keep this 9 p.m. curfew since you are older and more responsible.) When a boundary is no longer useful or helpful, it is eliminated. It is an ongoing process of communication and adjustment to keep the right boundary balance throughout the family stages.

Even when we are committed to setting healthy family boundaries, problem areas surface and need to be taken care of. Here is a guide for working out family boundaries that lead to connection rather than creating barriers to family relationships. We suggest you have the family sit down together to consider and interact around the following points.

□ Are there any complaints about physical, emotional or spiritual boundaries of any particular family member?

□ Have everyone express their personal needs and desires concerning this boundary.

□ Discuss the impact of that boundary on other family members.

□ Brainstorm together the ways that needs could be met should the boundary be changed.

□ Clarify the need for accountability if there is a change.

□ Try the new boundary to see how it works.

□ Continue to evaluate and make changes until everyone is satisfied.

These guidelines worked for the Piper family in this way. For many years the Pipers had a family rule that no one was to have phone calls after 10:00 p.m. As the children got older and their nights became longer, this rule became harder and harder to abide by. Especially when the kids came home from college for vacations and summers, the rule became a frustration for everyone. Don and Boni were frustrated to have calls coming into the house when they needed their sleep. Their children, young adults with good friends in different time zones, were frustrated with an antiquated rule.

Discussing the situation as a family made it clear that the rule needed to be changed. As family members expressed their needs (parents' for sleep, young adults' for contact with friends), the family loosened the boundaries. The kids asked their friends to be more sensitive to time zones; when they are at home and the phone rings late at night, they dash for it so they will not disturb the rest of the family members; Don and Boni have found that unplugging the bedroom phone makes it easier to ignore the ringing.

Centered in Christ
In this chapter we have spent a great deal of time describing how rightful degrees of cohesion, adaptability and boundaries help develop autonomous and responsible adult children. We do not mean to glorify an autonomy that leads to narcissistic, self-centered or self-serving persons. Rather we hope to develop children with a responsible sense of self so they can be rightly related to others. Created to be in

relationship with God and others, we have been given intellect and emotion to help us in this process. To the extent that we act out of self choices, we become the master of our souls. Connecting our head and our heart gives us capacity to respond to others in appropriate and creative ways. Self-talk and emotion-talk give us the balance of awareness and calmness. This helps us resist reactionary (out-of-control) anger or cold (overly controlled) detachment.

The concept of being centered in Christ gives us a core moral base from which to make responsible choices. Having access to and using all our senses (body), feelings (affect) and cognition (mind) help us make the kind of connection that sustains relationships. Paying attention to our whole self teaches us how to live in mutual giving and receiving relationships. Our affect gives us a passion to do for others, to recognize needs, to understand a person's plight. When we stay oblivious to others, we feel little obligation for our fellow human beings. By paying attention to our emotional side we are urged to see others with compassion, and by collaborating with our cognitive side we have wisdom to take responsible action.

Being centered in Christ means that we are dependent on God for validation. We check out what is right in God's sight, so we are driven by neither self needs nor others' needs alone but make choices out of a desire to please God.

Interdependence is a place where we are not determined by other people's demands or our own comfort but by mutual desires and reciprocal interaction. We put a priority on nurture and connection as well as independence and separation. We have freedom in Christ to risk condemnation and disapproval of others, because we gauge our behaviors on God's Word rather than on what others think or want. We make choices that are right in God's sight.

To help our children be centered in Christ, we must allow sufficient space for teens to become their own persons. Parents must forgo the right to claim time and energy without consulting them. We must respect our adult children's judgment and right to make mistakes. We must believe that they are capable of facing their own pain and working through their struggles without our intervention unless it is requested.

This process must begin in childhood, long before the leaving home begins. It is there that our children learn to feel connected in significant ways. They also learn to allow for change and flexibility within the family. And even very young children have a need to know that their boundaries are respected and will be honored by the adults in their lives. When children have a balance of connection, adaptability and clear boundaries as they are growing up, leaving home will not be fearful for them or their parents. Knowing we have been working toward this goal throughout their lives, we will be able to accept their new freedom as hoped-for growth.

Believing we can do nothing other than entrust our kids to God's care, we need to let them establish lives of their own that reflect their ideas and values. We empower them to be centered in Christ by helping them to see their worth in God's sight and to have purpose and meaning through faith in God. Empowered in Christ, they are new people, free to make wise and foolish choices, free to succeed and fail, free to rejoice in moments of triumph and moments of despair as children of God. We continue to empower them through our prayers, support and continual love and by letting them find their way in Christ. We relinquish them to their Lord.

Exercises

Now that you have determined what quadrant your family is in on the model given in this chapter, take some time to discuss with your adult child the dimensions of adaptability and connection. Talk about the impact it has on your current relationship and what adjustments could be made during this leaving-home phase of life. Make three concrete suggestions about changes that would improve your relationship.

Plan a private family ritual for your adult child's leaving-home day. Involve all family members (time, place, experience) when you create the event. Keep a surprise element (like choosing symbols) to make it more enjoyable. Perhaps you will decide to end the time with special foods, a memory book of photos, home movies or a prayer of blessing to make it a good goodby.

4

Empowerment Makes a Difference

....

I*s there a person in your life who believes in you when you lack* the confidence to believe in yourself? Do you have someone who helps you get beyond your self-imposed limitations? Did you have a parent, teacher, grandparent, relative or friend who guided and equipped you to develop your full potential? If you answer yes to these questions, then you know what it is to be empowered. Remembering this person will undoubtedly bring a smile to your lips and a warm feeling in your heart because you are acutely aware of what a difference empowerment makes in your life.

Take a moment to remember the special things this person did to empower you. Perhaps it was someone who encouraged you when you felt inadequate, supported you in reaching your goals or saw gifts and potential in you that were hidden from your view. For many people the empowering person was one who not only loved but also challenged and confronted them to climb to higher places. We are incredibly thankful for those who have stretched our horizons and helped us to be all that God created us to be.

I (Judy) remember Elzina with such fondness. She was a middle-aged single woman in my church who approached me during my teenage years. "Judy, I've noticed your leadership ability in the youth group. I believe you could write an article for the Christian magazine I edit. Would you be willing to try? I'll help you in any way I can."

I was flabbergasted that she had that kind of confidence in me, but most of all I was astounded that she thought I could do such a thing. The inner thrill of that attention guided me in the right direction. Not only was I validated by her request, but I soaked up the attention and special time Elzina spent helping me write an effective article. Forty years later I often think about the influence she has had on my professional career. She was certainly an empowerer.

Perhaps you named your parents as empowerers. Isn't this the highest compliment a child could give a parent? To be placed on our children's list of empowerers would affirm the part we have played in preparing them to leave home confidently.

Because we believe the concept of empowerment is essential to a good leaving-home experience, we devote this chapter to it. We first define empowerment, then give practical suggestions about how to be an empowering parent, and finally advocate the principle of being empowered in Christ.

What Is Empowerment?
Power can be defined as the ability to influence others. Influence can be a negative or positive force in a person's life. Power that is used for the good of others engenders growth, but power that is used to control others stymies growth. Coercive power keeps children ineffective, undetermined and overly dependent on their parents. Empowerment develops effective, responsible young adults.

Empowerment starts with the recognition that your child is uniquely gifted by God to make a significant mark in his or her world. Whether a child is able-bodied or developmentally challenged, female or male, black or white, he or she has a sacred purpose that can be achieved only by him or her. By affirming the specific strengths, talents and giftedness in each child, parents help their children develop in their own ways, in their own time and according to their own personality.

Personality and temperamental differences help us see that there are many ways of expressing one's self. Parents who view differences as resources rather than deficits delight in each child's particular contribution. They resist placing expectations on them to be like an older sister or a younger brother or their parents. This all-encompassing approach lessens competition between siblings and unrealistic expectations of parents.

A second aspect of empowerment is assisting children in age-appropriate ways so they can develop according to their own time frame. Children feel comfortable when expectations are within their own timetable rather than prescribed by a predetermined timetable that only heightens their anxiety when they do not measure up. Pressure like this often leads to failure and stymies potential. What children need is reassurance and support for the tasks they accomplish at their particular pace.

Parenting for Empowerment
Research indicates that there are two basic styles of parental leadership. Some parenting focuses on developing a warm, positive relationship between parent and child. Another approach to parenting focuses on tasks and content (imparting beliefs, values and attitudes) that need to be completed and learned. In some cases parents are neglectful in both realms of parental leadership. They neither provide guidelines nor give emotional support to their children. These parents may be inadequate, apathetic or too self-concerned. Perhaps they have a difficult time showing love or discipline.

In an authoritarian home parents clearly demand obedience but fail to give adequate emotional support. Children are forced to comply with parental demands without asking questions or expressing their views. When they get away from their parents, they often get out of hand. Although permissive parents give plenty of warmth and love, these parents often fail to provide children with clear guidance or rules. Behavior that needs correction is ignored, no limits are set, and yet plenty of warm fuzzies are showered on children. These children have trouble figuring out how to behave with peers who are not always so affirming. They want guidance, so they often try to establish rules by trial and error. For example, Sandy came home later and later each night in a effort to get her parents to set limits. It was not good enough to hear them say they knew she would make the right decisions. She needed specific input from her parents.

As you can see, parenting includes giving guidance and support. Jesus provides us with a model of empowerment. He refused to use his power to control others, but he chose to serve them instead. Empowerment is an intentional, interpersonal process that helps the less powerful one become personally proficient. Empowerment involves a commitment by parents to guide, nurture, equip, love and prepare our children for God's purposes. Helping them develop their God-given potential requires a deep respect for each unique child and his or her particular potential. Parenting for empowerment goes beyond developing personal strengths for self purposes. It sets up the higher vision of developing competence so they can powerfully serve others.

Empowering Components

A secular way of defining power is to think of it as a commodity that has a limited supply. This leads to the false assumption that as children grow older and become more powerful, parental power is automatically reduced. Empowerment, however, is completely contrary to this notion, for it is the attempt to establish power in our children. It does not mean parents yield to the wishes of their children but that they are active and intentional in helping their children acquire personal power so they can become self-directed and take responsible actions.

Parents who empower children toward responsible interdependence prepare them to live as healthy adults, capable of taking increasing charge of their own lives as they mature while at the same time building and maintaining a strong network of healthy relationships with others, including family. Parents who breed unhealthy dependence or excessive control will diminish parental influence and thwart emotional connection with their children. Empowering includes the following elements.

☐ Assuring: "I'm on your side and I believe in you."

☐ Encouraging: "You have strengths, gifts and talents."

☐ Challenging: "I invite you to reach your potential."

☐ Equipping: "Here are the skills necessary to achieve success."

☐ Trusting: "I know you made a mistake, but I see you've learned from it."

In Tom's life a number of these empowerment components came together through the following incident. Tom was asked by his teacher to give a speech during a high-school assembly. He was thrilled that the teacher thought enough of him to ask, but he was also bombarded with doubts about whether he could pull off the task.

When he got home that night, he talked to his father, Jerry, about it. Jerry listened carefully as his son spoke with excitement about the idea but also hinted at his fears about this challenge. Jerry congratulated his son on the honor but also acknowledged his feelings of inadequacy. He gave his support by promising to read Tom's first draft and give him honest feedback. This response conveyed his belief in his son's ability to write a speech and provided active support that would help Tom achieve his goal.

A few days later Tom rather nervously handed the rough draft to Jerry but was reassured when Jerry carefully pointed out the strengths, asked questions that stimulated additional ideas and gave helpful suggestions about the phrasing of some sentences.

Tom appreciated the positive and insightful interaction with his dad. He was relieved that there had not been one degrading, negative criticism. Rather, his father equipped him through kind and concrete ideas that renewed his confidence to do a rewrite.

When he wanted to practice his speech, it was his dad he asked to listen to him. And Jerry not only listened with pride but also offered a few pointers about Tom's delivery. Then he expressed his congratulations on a job well done with a high-five gesture.

When Tom gave his speech the next day, he did so with self-satisfaction and confidence. Jerry had empowered his son toward success by giving needed guidance and personal support. When the applause came at the end of his speech, Tom was thrilled with the response. His work and effort paid off, building up his self-esteem. His teacher had given him an opportunity to develop his talent, and his father had empowered him to succeed. He took the credit for what he had done, but he also learned how important it is to have the support of significant people.

Things were a little different for Katherine, who grew up in a conservative Christian home with many rules to govern her behavior. She was an obedient child and a fairly good student in high school but did not learn what it means to be personally empowered. When it came time to go to college, she chose a school a thousand miles from her home and was amazed by her newfound freedom. But making her own decisions was a shaky, new experience for her. She was so overwhelmed by the new environment that she failed to make decisions that were in her best interests. By the end of her first semester she had flunked all of her courses and was put on probation.

Katherine moved back home to face angry and disappointed parents. She spent the next year working at the local mall and began dealing with issues with her parents in family therapy. She worked on being her own person, and they worked on empowering her in that direction. By the time another year had gone by, she was continuing with her college education at the nearby community college. Now Katherine could approach her life with more clarity, and her parents communicated their belief in her as she moved toward her goals. Two years later she graduated with honors from the university. Her parents' new belief in her ability to manage her life was the boost she had needed. It felt wonderful to know they were behind her and trusted her to make wise choices.

Empowerment Through Teaching, Modeling, Delegating

Parenting for empowerment involves three major tasks: teaching, modeling and delegating. We begin the empowering process the day our totally dependent babies come into our homes. In the beginning of their life we do a lot of loving, bonding and nurturing to let them know they are cherished. Steadfast love shows itself through our words and actions as we respond to their feelings and wishes and care for their basic needs. Knowing there is nothing they can do to diminish our commitment to them fosters their sense of security and well-being. Acceptance and trust provide the foundation for empowerment.

Building on love and acceptance, empowerment continues through teaching, modeling and delegating behaviors of parents. When we teach and model integrity and congruence, we build character in our children that solidifies their progress toward maturity and meaningful existence. Wanting our children to be proficient in caring for themselves, effective in their interpersonal relationships and content with their life's purpose requires that we learn to delegate. Until we let them take action, all the teaching and modeling we do will be to no avail. So that they are able to do what they are called upon to do and do it well, we must let them go to take their own action. We want them to be able to stand on their own and make their unique way in the world.

We (the Pipers) were challenged when our daughter Karlie decided to take a semester off from college and go to Africa to work in a mission. This was an expensive dream and a scary one for us. But Karlie was determined to go and to raise as much money as she needed to get there. She discussed her plans with us and asked for our input on how to plan for this trip. Together we figured the cost of travel, personal expenses, passports and health care preparation. We brainstormed together for possible sources of income, and Karlie worked long hours at her summer job.

When we came up with an idea, we turned it over to Karlie. She took charge and made the decision whether to follow through on the idea. It was her adventure, her dream and her need to earn money. We believed she could do it and challenged her to find a way to fulfill her dream. Through a variety of ways, she reached her financial goal, took care of an enormous number of details and found herself on her way to Africa.

Some parents are particularly good at modeling behavior but not very good at teaching or giving the reasons certain behavior is expected. Other parents give a lot of instruction and advice, but their lives do not jibe with what they say. Parents who give good answers along with modeling the values and moral they adhere to give children a sound basis for their beliefs. An empowering mode is one in which parents teach by word and deed. Discipling involves leading persons through their thoughts, feelings and actions into a positive way of living.

Teaching for Empowerment

Not long after our children are born we begin using the teaching mode. We explain that they should not touch the hot stove or they will get burned, we tell them stories of how Jesus loves little children and in myriad ways give them knowledge that empowers. If you have ever been to a museum or a zoo, you are likely to observe parents in the fine art of the teaching their children. Take a moment to listen to the explanations given to their children, segments often read off the exhibit placards. Early childhood is that wonderful time when natural curiosity opens up a wealth of information about the world. Children seem to have an endless capacity to take in an enormous amount of teaching.

Teaching as empowerment can be an exciting and rewarding interaction between children and parents, especially if it is experienced as a time of enjoyment and intrigue. However, if parents are obsessed with pouring information into their children so they will do well in school or be accepted by prestigious schools, learning soon becomes coercive and disempowering. Perfectionism or daunting expectations block learning and disrupt the parent-child relationship. Power is corrupted when parents are motivated by their own desire rather than having the best interest of their child in mind.

I (Judy) have a regretful memory of disempowering my nine-year-old daughter while teaching her how to play the piano. My standing over her while she practiced until she got it right was an exasperating experience for both of us. Being overly invested in her achievement at the piano because of my family's musical background, I failed to recognize her discomfort and disinterest in fulfilling my dreams. I was unable to let her discover the joy of music in her own way. I will never forget that painful night of her piano recital, sitting in the audience with her grandparents. She panicked during her performance, forgot her notes and left the stage in tears. She was trying to be perfect for us, and that is not empowerment. She has since forgiven me for those disempowering actions, but how often I wish I could redo those moments.

Consequent to this experience I was directed to the parent effectiveness training material, where I learned the amazing power of natural and logical consequences. Natural consequences are based on letting the natural flow of events take place without a parent's interfering or rescuing. For example, when your daughter is caught speeding, she is obligated by the law to either pay the speeding ticket or lose her driver's license.

Logical consequences are based on the parent and adult child's arranging a consequence that is logical in nature and agreed on ahead of time. For example, you and your son agree that should he get an F in a college course, he will have to pay to retake the course. The advantage of setting up logical consequences is that it avoids a power struggle, eliminates unnecessary parental interference and teaches children to take responsibility for their actions. Discovering a new approach to parenting was a tremendous relief that led to a transformation in our home. The empowering principles made all the difference. High respect and encouragement that lead them to be responsible for their behavior are the secrets to producing competent, self-determined children.

Teaching children the wonderful facts of life so they will have a deeper understanding about the world is an incredible privilege. And learning together is an effective way to empower through teaching. One summer Jack and Judy vacationed for three weeks in Colorado and Arizona with their grandchildren Curtis (ten) and Jacob (nine). What fun we had together visiting museums, climbing mountains, playing games at night and reading a special book about the Navajo Indians before going to sleep. Mutual empowerment occurred as we answered their curious questions and discovered God's world together.

Modeling for Empowerment

No doubt about it! Children learn more by watching their parents model values and character than they do by listening to what their parents tell them. When modeling and teaching go together, they have a tremendous impact on children. If we are empowered persons, our children will learn a vast amount by watching us tackle life's challenges. They will see us make mistakes and learn from them. They will notice how relying on a belief in God and a support system of family and friends helps us get beyond our fears and limitations. When we are in sync with ourselves, our children will value congruence in themselves.

When our kids see us as overly cautious, fearful, self-doubting and incompetent, that rubs off too. If we paint a bleak, pessimistic picture of life, it will be difficult for our children to have a positive vision for themselves. It is difficult for kids to get beyond the limitations and barriers of their parents. Unless we have a solid sense of self, our children will be unable to develop theirs. Our inhibitions will inhibit them. If we want to be a positive influence on their growth, we must work on our growth. If you have a tendency to be unsure of yourself, overly dependent or controlling, it is a signal to you that you have your own work to do. The sooner you can do this, the more likely you will be able to empower your own children.

Modeling is our most effective influence, for when our lives are congruent with our teaching it is living proof that beliefs and actions go together. Parents are like player-coaches who participate in activities with their children. They instruct by modeling the desired behavior. When our children witness us taking responsibility for consequences of our actions, it shows them that integrity comes through addressing our failures as well as our successes. When children move into their preteen years, they have developed many abilities but may lack confidence to attempt more independent action. If we participate with children in tasks and responsibilities and take the initiatives necessary to motivate them, that helps them to develop courage to function on their own. This process is how one empowers through modeling. The amount of parent input is lessened as a child moves toward responsible independence. Here is where parents must learn to delegate.

Delegating for Empowerment

Wise parents delegate. Although modeling influences our children throughout life, during this last stage of parenting we need to do less teaching and more delegating. As our children approach preteen and teenage years, they learn best by making decisions on their own and by taking personal responsibility for the consequences of their actions. They are now developing their own ideas, feelings and thoughts and are much more influenced by their peers and other adults.

By the time children reach this stage, we are no longer telling them what to do because they are now doing it for themselves. Little control or parental involvement is needed. Now we ought to have confidence in their ability to take on tasks without our help. For example, a college student is quite able to pack his or her own things for college. While Mother and Father might offer to carry a few things to the car or send a surprise package of cookies along for the trip as gestures of affection, it is clearly unsuitable to do their packing for them.

The hardest thing about delegating is letting go. Sometimes parents may need to give their children a gentle nudge out of the nest so they can spread their wings and learn to fly. If we fail to give our blessing for the flight, they may never dare leave the nest. When leaving is overdue, the thought of spreading their wings becomes an even more fearful idea. They may falter during their first solo flight, but unless they take that risk they will never be empowered to soar. Like the mother eagle that pushes her baby over the edge of the nest but glides beneath to catch it when it falters, empowering parents delegate responsibility, step back and allow their children to make their own decisions. We will be there to lend a supporting hand if they falter, but only after they have taken flight.

Let children make mistakes? How can we stand back and watch them move toward disaster? We want to protect them because we are acutely aware of the grave consequences of even one mistake. However, if they are frozen by an inability to make choices or have an inordinate need for safety, this is another kind of tragedy. Life teaches us from the mistakes we make so we will not repeat them. We can do no other than let our adult children make choices, even when they are mistaken choices. We can help them think through their choices by asking good questions, acknowledging the fearfulness of adult responsibility and believing they have what it takes to meet their personal challenges. In order to help them reach their potential, we need to stretch beyond our own fears or thoughts that they cannot make it without us. We instill courage in our children to meet the risky ventures of life not by refusing to let them fly but by refusing to let them try.

Parents are empowered in the process of empowering their children. We learn mutual respect and regard for each other. Through the parenting pilgrimage we teach, model and delegate in order to empower them to live competent, responsible and enriching lives.

Empowering, Not Enabling

Enabling as a concept has become synonymous with codependency, which is a flawed dependency on others that comes out of one's own need to be needed. Unable to stand on his or her own, the enabler fails to challenge others, so they never become accountable for their actions. Covering up, denying and going along with destructive actions are behaviors referred to as *enabling*. Taking this term into the parent-child relationship, we believe that sometimes parents are overly hooked into their relationship with their children because of their own dependency needs. Therefore they tend to encourage immature instead of mature behavior.

Let's look at the implications of enabling behavior. When you think about it, it is the opposite of the empowerment principle, for it attempts to control rather than grow children. Instead of accepting or respecting an adult child's decisions, parents who are enablers use shaming messages to obligate their children to do what the parents want them to do. Instead of helping their children think through their own ideas, the parents encourage their children to think, feel and act as they do, and the children are kept dependent. Parents who are enablers discourage competency. If children think or act on their own, these parents have worked themselves out of a job and feel useless.

Adult children who are unable to establish a vision for themselves end up being trapped into doing things to please others. Interdependency is empowering, but teenagers who are overly dependent fail to take responsibility for the consequences of their actions on others. They begin to take on the role of a victim with no choices. They blame others for their unhappiness or lack of personal success. Being unsure of oneself and feeling incapable of making a meaningful choice opens that person to manipulation, coercion and control by others. These dependent teenagers do not stand on their own two feet, but worse than that, they do not have the slightest idea how to stand on their own. Their decisions about career, mate and other life choices become a matter of not deciding. They lack power and energy to make things happen for themselves.

The Shaming Aspect of Parenting
When academic achievement is the top priority of parents, it is extremely difficult to remain silent when a daughter neglects studies to spend an inordinate amount of time practicing cheerleading drills. In such a case it's tempting to use guilt or shame to keep her in conformity with your values. Brittany complains, "The closer I get to making my own decisions, the more my parents batter me with their accusations of disloyalty." This young woman is extremely frustrated at her parents for trying to control her through guilt trips. These shaming messages disrupt the emotional connection and empowerment process.

Already encumbered with feelings of self-doubt and inadequacy, adolescents are painfully vulnerable to parental disapproval or ridicule. Lack of sensitivity, expressions of anger or even well-intentioned criticism can put a youth over the edge. Responding with contempt, blame or humiliation takes a tremendous emotional toll, for interpersonal shame reverts to an internal shame of insufficiency. The experience of rejection sets into motion a chain of shaming patterns that repeat themselves from generation to generation.

In shaming homes family members set up a standard of perfection that is impossible to achieve. The strong focus on external behavior impedes a person's internal development. Members not only fear making mistakes but also believe they are a mistake, thinking they can never be good enough. In the innermost part of their being, they are ashamed of who they are. Discouraged by failing to live up to unreasonable standards, they give up. With a deep sense of disgrace, they become hopeless and defeated. Though it may be their only defense, blaming themselves or others for their predicament leads to further problems and irresponsible behavior. How do parents move beyond shaming tactics and toward self-affirming empowerment?

The first thing parents must do to help children recover from shaming is to acknowledge fault and ask for forgiveness. By risking such vulnerability we model humility and a willingness to make amends that lead to restored relationship. If we believe that covering up failure is a barrier to closeness, we will have reason enough to reveal ourselves. When we are most ourselves, when our children see who we are, they see us as human. If we tell our secrets, our children will find connection through our common humanness. When we admit to our weaknesses as well as our strengths, God uses these moments to bring us close. The truth telling of our own stories becomes the doorway to healing and empowerment. Our journey can become a witness and a source of wisdom for our children. We have a story to tell. They need to hear us convey how God continues to transform and restore our lives so they will be drawn to the Savior.

An empowered person is free of shame and full of potential. You no longer have to be something you are not. Whereas self-judgment stymies vitality, self-assurance builds up potential. A healthy spiritual core rather than a toxic shame core integrates one's internal life with interpersonal connection. Having one's meaning and purpose centered in Christ means we look to the One who is greater than ourselves for strength.

Empowering Grace
To forgive and be forgiven is the hallmark of the Christian family. Yet we know many families often live under the cloud of shame rather

than grace. The discouragement incurred in a shaming home defeats the hopeful message of God's grace. God so loved and cherished each unique created being that he gave his only Son for them. The intent was to restore and reconcile. Likewise, a family of grace will embrace each member as a unique, cherished creation of God. While they acknowledge human failure, they also take hope in the capacity for one to learn from mistakes and recover from imperfections. Repentance and forgiveness become redeeming ways to reconciliation, hope and life. Only when family members are loved, accepted and forgiven do they have the courage to begin anew.

Empowered by God
Empowerment is a biblical principle. Being created in the image of God, our children have the potential to become what God intends them to be. They have the capacity to go beyond human limitations by looking to the Holy Spirit to empower them to live abundant lives in Christ. Life goals then are made in the context of biblical norms and expectations. Parents can encourage this growth by noticing changes, pointing out progress and paying attention to times of reaching out to others and of making personal sacrifices. Empowerment happens when we challenge faulty thinking and actions, point out consequences of behavior and help our children find ways that are in keeping with God's directives. Offering a spiritual meaning to life helps them learn to depend on God to reach their goals. It is much easier to let go when we depend on God's action in their lives.

Depending on God as a source of maturity is what we call being empowered in Christ. Knowing, trusting and becoming obedient to God's way is the true path to maturity. It is God's Spirit who prompts the heart and provides the strength to turn a cheek, ask for forgiveness, stand up for righteous causes and speak out boldly for one's convictions. God's validation rather than self-validation, parent validation or peer validation is the goal. Choosing God's ways rather than one's own way or somebody else's way is the key to fulfillment. When our adult children have an identity that is firmly planted in Christ, they can grasp the deeper spiritual meaning of who they are and what they do. It is Jesus who ultimately changes our life, heals our wounds, draws us to himself and empowers us to follow a godly path. While human relationships within the family challenge and shape us, it is God who convicts and gives us the spiritual power to change.

If we want our young people to reach their potential for God, we must risk the discomfort that sometimes comes with challenging behavior that we believe leads them away from God's way. We must be honest and direct with our feelings, thoughts and desires as we work through the rough places of disagreement with our children. We must be ready and willing to give input that stretches their thinking and expands their views. Demanding compliance without explanation usually results in rebellion and rejection of our ideas. But when we offer our viewpoint, we do so with the hope that they will be able to integrate our input with their ideas because they are open to what we have to say. Since we believe that choices made in line with God's divine principles will reap rewards, just as selfish and controlling actions will reap havoc, we need a forthright and honest exchange with our children. By grappling with our children on an issue, we show them love and a vital involvement in their lives. While young adults must make their own choices and be responsible for their lives, parents must actively contribute their thoughts, feelings and caring without fail. To do any less would do them a great disservice.

During times when our basic beliefs are at odds, we are obliged to express our concerns. Bringing in an objective person (pastor, counselor, friend) is often a great help in this particular situation. I (Judy) remember when my parents and I met with a pastoral counselor because of differences about the church I was attending. My mother had serious concerns about some of the spiritual practices that I had found meaningful to my spiritual growth. The argument between us became so heated we could not get through it alone. The gentle, caring pastor who met with our family at this time of turmoil was extremely helpful. He provided a safe place for me to express my spiritual enthusiasm and also helped me listen to my parents, who wanted me to worship with them at our home church. Without dampening my spirit or disrespecting my parents, he helped us find an acceptable compromise. I remember the angry tears streaming down my face at the beginning of our meeting and the peace that was present at the end of that meeting. In this case the pastor brought light to a dark situation.

When parents and adult children try to work out differences, it is imperative that both sides give up idyllic expectations or defensive postures so that dialogue is possible. Parents need to offer ideas of hope that both challenge and enrich their children. We need to hear each other out and step back from our biases, opinions and sacred stances so we can really listen to each other with understanding. Sometimes, out of our desire to have our children turn out a certain way, our vision is clouded. When we look to God for wisdom, it is amazing what can happen.

God's power is nurturing power. Flowing from his loving concern, God's power empowers us to relate to others in like manner. The task of parenting is to help our children know themselves as persons of God who are capable of making covenants with others. Just as God holds us accountable for our actions, parents hold their children to a similar accountability. Discipline encourages children to take responsibility for their actions, helps them to be reliable, empathic and responsive to others and maximizes their potential to be children of God. Self-congruency and internal security give our children the capacity to accomplish satisfying goals, forgive themselves and others, affirm their abilities, value personal needs and find meaning in their lives. This honest, empowering relationship with our children prepares them for leaving home as responsible adults.

Mutual empowerment is grounded in love. Being centered in Christ empowers young people to act out of a place that keeps both the good of others and care for themselves in a rightful balance. Caring for oneself is necessary to rightly love and give oneself to others. When family members use their power for each other they will know the riches that comes from family living. The hope (Col 1:27) for our children is Christ in them, moving them toward maturity in the wisdom and knowledge of God. If we are rooted and built up in Christ, established in the faith and empowered by the Holy Spirit's power, there is promise of bearing one another's burdens, showing compassion, kindness, humility, meekness, patience and forgiving one another (Col 3:12-21). The family is a sacred place in which members celebrate a common meaning and purpose that is beyond themselves. Anchored in Christ, the family works, lives, worships and has their being in Christ Jesus.

Exercise

List all the ways empowering takes place in your home. Discuss together whether any enabling is being done in your family. Decide what you can do to increase mutual empowerment, and make an effort this week to do one or two empowering acts each day. If this is a good experience, keep it up.

5

On Their Own & in Transition

....

Remember that leaving-home picture we had you imagine in chapter one? Now imagine your adult child in his or her home away from home. Whether that new home is a room in a college dorm, a military barracks or an apartment building, your adult child is living somewhat independently. One of the major developmental tasks ahead of him or her is to establish self-definition and direction in this new environment. As your children are open to a variety of lifestyle choices, it can be quite a struggle for them to accomplish this task and a struggle for parents as we look on. How do we learn to support them from afar during this transition time as well as live with them when they visit?

Especially on those return visits, we will be challenged with new behaviors and beliefs that are likely to push our buttons. How will we discern what responses are detrimental and which ones might be helpful? First we will look at the various situations our adult children find themselves in when they leave our home. Then we will look at typical difficulties that arise and interactions that will further their growth and our relationship with them.

A Time of Transition

Young people make so many adjustments when they leave home for the first time. Some have never had to share a bedroom, and most have not shared a room with someone other than a family member. Apartment living means getting along with a limited amount of space, learning to get along with a housemate and dealing with strangers who live next door. Privacy is minimal in the college dorm or at the military barracks. These young adults herd together with other young adults, showering, eating, playing and studying en masse. For many youths such transitions are desirable and exhilarating; for others the transitions are painful and disconcerting. However, most will work hard to adjust to their new surroundings and learn to fit in the best way they can. They will flex their independence muscles, establish new boundaries and develop a support system apart from their family. Many do this well. Others find it a nightmare and cannot seem to adjust, no matter how hard they try. Where do we as parents fit in to help them succeed?

No Place Like Home

There are as many different responses to going away and coming home as there are adult children. Glenda recalls her dismay after she went away to college. Shut up in her dorm room, she wept over her feelings of not belonging. At seventeen she was not quite ready for this new venture, and she was literally sick about being away from home. Yet when she traveled back home during semester break, she instantly felt out of place there as well. Life had gone on without her. Routines and schedules were different. There was an empty remoteness about the bedroom that had been the center of her life and friendships when she was in high school. "I was frazzled! Nothing was the same, and I no longer belonged there either. I shut the door and sobbed over my feelings of displacement. How would I even find a home or sense of belonging again?" She felt like Dorothy in Oz, looking for a home, scared she would not know how to get there. The experience left her frightened and disoriented for the first two years of college.

This is quite a common response in the in-between time of leaving home and moving out of the home. Whether one is off to college, work or military service, the question is similar: Where do I really belong? When a young adult's belonging is not yet clearly established outside the home, it is easy to get knocked off one's feet during that passage from the old to the new. Besides that, change is occurring in both places at the same time. Not having a secure foothold in either place, young people feel that the ground is moving beneath their feet.

Living in Their Own Place
In spite of the excitement involved in having a child leave home, there is usually apprehension on the part of both adult children and their parents. Are they really ready? Is this the right choice for them? How will they manage without us? Will they find the right kind of friends? are a few of the haunting questions going through their minds. In addition one of the usually unspoken concerns of our adult children is that they will lose their place in the family. This can be a hard thing to talk about. It is not as if they are not looking for change, but they want to control the changes that come. Children in college are in an in-between stage of leaving home. Most consider the family home to still be their true place of residence and want the family to hold their place there.

My (Boni, who will be speaking throughout this chapter unless otherwise noted) friend Kathy's son called home from college to find that his parents had given his room to a friend of the family. Todd was upset. No one had asked him if this person could stay in his room. Kathy had not been aware of how significant this would be to Todd, and it gave them a good opportunity to talk.

It is a good sign to our adult children when we intentionally keep their rooms intact so they have a familiar place to come home to during the first few years out of the home. They are not ready to have their family move on too quickly without them. Keep in mind that during this transitional time, it helps if they can look back to the familiar as they forge ahead into new territory. Knowing they have a special place in their family when they come back helps them surge forward.

When children move quickly out of the home without going through a transition period after high school, they may appear to have made more developmental progress than they have. While setting up a home of their own may be exciting for them, they are often not ready to let go of the home they shared with their family. Even though they may establish a living arrangement away from home, they usually will not want you to move on too quickly without them. Gary wanted to leave part of his belongings at home just in case things did not work out with a new roommate. Jeanette asked her mother to help decorate the apartment she was sharing with her friend but did not want her to make any changes in her bedroom at home. Some will ask to have their bedroom set or other miscellaneous pieces of furniture to help furnish their new place of residence.

College students often have the benefit of parental support in various forms. Their leaving home may happen more gradually than does the leaving of those entering military life or getting their own apartment. Yet the pressures they feel are sometimes overwhelming. Juggling the academic demands, part- or full-time work expectations and a social life can be an enormous challenge for many young adults. Our support and stability can make the difference in their success or failure.

The Military Scene

Let's take some time to consider the dynamics of many who leave home early to enter the military. Those born in the 1970s and early 1980s, referred to as Generation X, tended to grow up in homes where parents hesitated to impose much structure on them. The average amount of time spent with both parents declined, and fathers spent even less time with their children than did fathers in prior generations. The high divorce rate suggests these kids spent much of their growing-up years being cared for by surrogate caretakers. Some of this generation experienced unmet belonging needs that led them to an early exit from home. Perhaps feeling lonely, isolated and lacking family connection, they were searching for a niche to make up for deficits of their growing-up years.

One way to find security is to join the military service. This institution promises to provide for basic needs, to train and to offer a sense of meaning. Some youth may be attracted to military life for this reason. The slogan "Be all that you can be in the Army" is a great incentive to find oneself. Perhaps looking for a surrogate family of sorts, these young people are also given what they need: a clear hierarchy and structure as well as a place of belonging. The disciplinary role of the officers gives enlisted men and women the clarity of rules they may have found lacking in their homes. Besides this, they now have a mission beyond themselves in serving their country.

The initial attraction to the military may dwindle if one's needs for emotional connection, bonding and nurture are not met in that environment. The majority of young enlisted men get married soon after basic training. Perhaps they hope to find a different source of emotional bonding from what the military offers. Unfortunately, many of them lack the maturity to sustain their marriages, a fact that presents them with further problems. For others the military is just what is needed to transition from dependency to independency. We can attest to how this happened for Nat as we listen to his story.

It has not been easy, he admits, but he learned some valuable lessons that have matured him through four years in the navy. Nat was trained as a cook and stationed on a submarine, the USS *Bremerton*. Cooking was a new skill that he thoroughly enjoyed, and he won commendation from the officers for his creative recipes. His commanding officer affirmed his skills, and this affirmation gave him further incentive to become a chef. Nat plans to attend a well-known chef school when sea duty is over.

Things have not always gone smoothly for Nat in the military. There were months when his commitment to Christ was shaken, and his choices did not always reflect obedience. The prayers of his church family and friends were answered, and Nat renewed his commitment to his Lord during his military stint. He praises God for bringing him to repentance and back to a heart centered on God. Other blessings followed. He listened to those who advised that he remain single instead of getting into a premature marriage. He took seriously the idea that he could develop himself through such activities as journaling, learning skills in communication and conflict resolution, eating and exercising properly, deepening his spiritual life, joining the basketball team, doing a good job in his role as cook.

Nat began to save money rather than spend it foolishly, and now he has enough for his education and even some for a future marriage. Being intentional about his faith, he spent many hours in Bible reading and reflection, led a Bible study with a few other shipmates and had a rich prayer life. This was one important way of staying close to those he loved at home, he claimed. His best buddy at home and he felt a deep connection in their faith that will last a lifetime.

The chaplain on board asked Nat to be worship leader for Protestant services during those long sea deployments. This surprised and pleased Nat and was used to further develop his leadership skills. He enriched his life with travel and an appreciation for people of different cultures and faiths. After these four years in the military, a rather immature adolescent has become a mature young man.

The Transitional Storm

Many young adults make the transition into adulthood, thriving on their choices and learning from their mistakes. They meet the challenging struggle, manage to weather the storm of transition and learn to do what it takes to make it. The experience has matured and prepared them for making it on their own. For others the transition from dependency to independence proves to be their breaking point. How do we as parents respond to this transition time? The question for us is how to interact with our children during visits home in ways that contribute to a smooth and mutually gratifying transition.

Back at the Ranch

After our children have left home, we go on with our lives. Then we start counting the days until that first visit home. We anticipate the return of our child on holidays, even if they live within a few miles from us. We have visions of the good old days when the family is all together again. We tend to forget about the changes that have already occurred and the extra stress during the holiday seasons that may make this visit less than ideal. Here is an example of what kind of clashes can happen during those reunions.

Julie, a young friend of ours, spent her first year of college in California, a thousand miles away from home. Her first trip home came at Christmas. Her mother, Tina, was beside herself with excitement. She bought the ingredients for all of Julie's favorite meals and treats before her arrival. In addition Tina scheduled several family events that Julie had always loved. Tina was sure Julie would be delighted by all her efforts.

Much to her chagrin, Tina was stunned by Julie's response. After the first few hours of expressing how good it was to be home again, the honeymoon of Julie's first visit home was over. During the meal together that night, Julie announced she was on a low-fat diet and could not bring herself to eat those fat-laden desserts her mother had so lovingly prepared. To be truthful, Julie was appalled by her mother's lack of nutritional knowledge. Since she was on the verge of becoming vegetarian, Julie said she could not stomach the favorite meals of juicy hamburgers, roasts and ribs. She made it clear that she would prefer cooking for herself on her own timetable: "I'm not used to eating on someone else's schedule and don't want to be tied down to a family dinnertime. Thanks anyway, but I'll manage on my own." It was like a slap in the face to Tina.

To make things even worse, the events that Tina had worked so hard to arrange were pooh-poohed. Julie was not about to spend all her free time with relatives. She was no longer interested in those things and elected not to go. She had friends to see and places to go that did not include her family. There were other irritating habits as well. Wearing wrinkled clothes, sleeping at odd hours, staying up half the night and rarely picking up after herself were behaviors the family had not expected.

"Who is this person?" moaned Tina. "She isn't the daughter who left home just four months ago. How could she have changed so drastically in such a short time!" With an eagerness similar to what she felt as she awaited Julie's coming home, she now awaited her return to school. "I can't wait for her to leave so the rest of us can get back to normal," she confided. "What happened to her?"

Julie is exploring many possible changes for herself, and the whole family will feel the impact of these changes. Furthermore, the entire family is changing as well. Members are changing simultaneously, for one member cannot change without the others changing at the same time. Entrances and exits bring instability. The void left by the young adult's absence must be filled in other ways. The entire family rearranges itself to deal with the gaps in order to find a new balance and stability. The movement in the family is like steps in a dance. Each member learned a pattern of steps while living together, but when one member is no longer part of that dance, the others readjust and create a new dance.

To elaborate on the matter of simultaneous change, let's consider another factor that contributes to how a particular family may react to the changes that occur. Think of the four unbalanced family styles (chapter three). Each of these families will undoubtedly respond in a different way to our friend Julie when she comes home for vacation. You will see a wide variety of dances that are created by each of these family styles.

In the rigid home Julie will be in big trouble right off if she assumes she will be able to translate her free choices at college with equally free behaviors at home. After all, there are strict rules to abide by, and everyone knows exactly what will be expected of her during a holiday visit. Julie's obedience to the family traditions and rituals will be strictly enforced. She will keep her room neat, iron her clothes and be present for dinner as expected. What she had been doing at college the last several months will not disrupt this family routine. She will probably be relieved when vacation is over so she can be free to make personal choices again. Now that she's home, the family puts her back into the role she had before she left. The family is attempting to deny the change and to keep her from expressing her change in the family dance. The longer she is away, the more difficult it will be to remain the same.

If Julie were part of an enmeshed home, family closeness would be the priority. For Julie this will mean her newfound independence is unacceptable. To act on her own behalf will be treated as disloyalty to the family. She will be expected to participate in all family activities, and any inclination to the contrary is a disgrace. Being primed in college to think more independently will cause her tension as she swallows her own thoughts to keep on track with the family beliefs. Smothered by a false sense of family togetherness, she begins to realize what it costs her to be part of this family.

In the chaotic family Julie will most likely experience a great deal of ambiguity during her vacation stay. What few rules there were may have already changed, and she will adjust or follow her own rules without much difficulty. Plans are sporadic, so when there is something to do the activity may include one or two members who are available at that time. Other family members will go their separate ways. Since change is such a regular part of this family dance, her personal steps in the dance do not cause much disruption, nor does she seem to make a difference there. This extreme flexibility results in many different dances going on at once, and she does not know exactly where she fits. It can be a lonely, disorienting experience because she does not seem to matter much to anyone. She is glad to return to college, where she is more comfortable with the structure provided by class schedules, study periods and planned social activities. In the college environment she matters to her friends and has a definite place of belonging.

In the disengaged family Julie will experience little connection among the members. Living separate lives is the norm, so it is unlikely that anyone will pay much attention to her eating preferences; everyone does as he or she pleases when it comes to food. There will be little protest about making independent plans, for there is little intentional family tradition. Julie will be free to go and come as she pleases, with few expectations. Julie begins to wonder why she came home, since there is little warmth or connection with other family members. Next vacation she will accept her roommate's invitation to spend time with her family. Julie senses that something is missing in her home.

As we consider these extreme scenarios, we can sense there is something wrong. Each of these families lacks the balance that is so crucial for personal growth toward independence. Each family is unable to help young people make the necessary transition due to the lack of cohesiveness between family members and a lack of healthy flexibility that promotes individuality. In a balanced family the members have created a new dance in your absence, but you are invited back into the dance when you return home. They will even help you learn the steps, so you can enter in and enjoy your new place in the dance. They are also eager to watch you dance your own dance and applaud you as you share your personal discoveries and changes. They have no need to keep you in the old routine, for they themselves have made changes that work well for the family in your absence.

In a balanced family Julie will be able to negotiate with other members about eating practices and family events. Personal boundaries are not only permitted but also carefully attended to and valued. Such a family expresses feelings and thoughts about issues between them so they can resolve differences and stay connected. There is a flexibility that accommodates Julie's needs and desires without taking away from the family's needs. Expressions of affirmation and respect continue to give Julie a sense of belonging along with a freedom of self-definition.

Another example of a balanced response comes from the Piper family during the first Christmas vacation Aaron came home for a visit. He responded quite differently than Julie did. In fact, he took great delight in knowing that things would be predictable. He hoped little had changed since his leaving. He wanted to watch every Christmas television special the family ever watched, all together again. He looked forward to traditional family outings and attended *The Nutcracker* and *A Christmas Carol* with enthusiasm. He hoped for every special meal to be prepared and all the old events to be held. It was important to him that many things stay constant. He is a sentimentalist and loves the feeling of the familiar.

But Aaron had changed too. It annoyed him that we wanted to know when he would be home and if he would be there for dinner. No one had asked him that for months. It was hard to be back in a family that had changed as well, closing in the gap his leaving created. He did not always appreciate it when the family expected familylike things from him. We needed to listen to each other to acknowledge the differences and respect the changes that had occurred. In the process of talking together, we found ways to loosen as well as maintain close relations.

It is good to remind yourself that each young adult is unique and will respond differently to situations. Allow for the differences, and do not try to compare your kids with each other or kids from other families. Talk with them about their unique perspective on things and make plans according to their desires and preferences. We will also consider some common areas of dispute and then offer some tips for getting along during those visits.

Whose Is What?

It is helpful for parents to discern which behaviors and beliefs of our children will directly affect the child and which will affect the parents. Will your daughter's habit of wearing wrinkled clothes affect you or her? Will your son's hairstyle affect you or him? Does clutter in one's bedroom affect the parents or the child? Choosing matters that really matter is the key. Parents must decipher the essential from the nonessential issues when deciding to give an opinion or question a behavior. Honest interaction about those things that really matter, rather than being caught up in trivial things, will minimize the conflict between you.

It can be difficult to separate our issues from those of our children, yet it is imperative we learn to do this in order to launch children who are independent. Ask yourself, *Is this my issue or my child's? Is it my hair, my clothes, my kitchen sink?* I knew it was not my hair or my clothes, but it was my kitchen sink. It made sense to negotiate at that point, because I was being affected by the mess in the kitchen that they were quite willing to live in. Their hair and what they chose to wear belonged to them. The kitchen sink belonged to the entire family. We all used that space in common, and it was important to respect that fact. Being able to distinguish between these areas minimized the conflict during this volatile developmental stage.

Negotiating the Territory
Negotiating the home territory when a child returns for visits can be a tricky business. The need to address boundaries (chapter three) is particularly important during these visits. Especially when college students come home for the summer break, it can be a testy time for families. College life is so different today compared with how things were in our generation. For example, college extracurricular activities may begin at ten at night or even later. When my daughter Karlie refereed volleyball games for a part-time job, many games began at midnight. For many college students, real life begins when most of us are sound asleep. This can take quite a toll on family life when our students come home for vacation. Negotiating these lifestyle differences is imperative. Just because your young adults are out half the night does not mean they are into trouble, as we might have thought in our day. But neither does it mean we cannot get any sleep for an entire summer. Talking adult to adult about both of your needs will usually work to bring about a compromise you can both live with.

In high school the Piper children had curfews appropriate to their ages. But the summer after high-school graduation was a no-curfew training time, giving them more freedom to set their own hours with guidance from us as needed. As each child worked during the summer months, we allowed them the freedom to determine for themselves when they would be in and out of the house. We expected them to make it to work and to be able to function on the job. We also expected them to take care of their health by getting sufficient sleep. When and if they did not do that, we reserved the right to talk with them about it, help them plan better or even reestablish a temporary curfew if necessary.

As each child tested the reality of no curfew by staying out quite late a few times, they also accepted the reality of needing to get up for work. There were times when we had to talk with them about their behavior when it was extreme, but that usually corrected the problem. They knew we did not want to monitor their hours and wanted them to take control in this area. They wanted that too, so our goals were the same, and together we were successful.

When connection and adaptability are balanced, we are better able to negotiate through this transitional time of our child's coming and going. We can discuss the old rules and not be afraid to establish new rules. We can hear of new friends, new beliefs and new dreams without feeling the threat of family disintegration. We can draw close and not fear separation.

Taking Off Masks

If parents or adult children feel the need to pretend that things are going well during home visits when they are not, they will never be able to deal effectively with the real issues. Home needs to be a place of protection where it's safe to let our masks down so we can honesty interact with one another.

How well I (Judy) remember the Christmas visit when things looked good on the surface. But for two full weeks I had sensed a tremendous tension between my parents. The night before I returned to college, everything broke loose between my parents when I observed a shouting match in the kitchen. It was all about us kids, the financial burden of college bills, the emotional closeness between my mother and me and my dad's anger and jealousy about that. I was devastated. That next semester my grades suffered through the worry I felt about their relationships. I wrote a story in English class about a couple's divorce during their daughter's first year away at college. I ended the story with this comment by the daughter: "It's all my fault! I'll never forgive myself for what's happened."

My parents did not divorce, but that incident was an example of trying to cover up rather than be honest. Hiding the truth never changes the truth. Keeping silence never alleviates the tension. Holding secrets never solves the problems. When masks are off, family members can deal openly with what is happening, sort out the truth and decipher what can be done so things will change. When the family is willing to grapple with the family pain, restoration is possible. Vitality comes out of open interactional rhythms that move the family toward growth.

Surviving Holidays: Tips for Parents

Holidays are a good opportunity for young adults to test their new beliefs and see the responses they bring from parents. Your children are home long enough for interaction to take place, but that time is short enough for it not to be overwhelming. Our young adult children need stable, nonreactive adults so they can test out their new ideas. It is important that we tolerate their thoughts and feelings in a way that shows respect and love. When we become a stable force for them to kick against, to tell the difference between our idea and their idea or where we begin and they leave off, we offer them a way to independence.

Do not presume what they are saying is written in stone. This is a time for young adults to test their beliefs. They do this by saying outrageous things, sometimes waiting to see what it sounds like on their lips and how it affects their parents' ears. A common one in the Piper household, where each of the children has gone to a Christian university costing fifteen to twenty thousand dollars a year, was "I don't think I believe in Christian education anymore." Resisting the urge to respond with "What! After all we've spent on you!" or "That shows what you know about anything!" I now (after three children) respond with "Really? Tell me what you're thinking about that."

You need to plan on them questioning whatever you value and learn to admire them for the courage that often takes. Respond with words that help them talk, and try not to react. They need to hear their own words; they do not need your reactionary outburst to confuse the issue.

Take into account the amount of freedom in their current situation. What restrictions has your son or daughter had these last months? Has he or she had a curfew? Mandatory classes? Meal check-ins? Some institutions still have these types of rules, but most do not.

Most likely your young adults have made their own choices about when to go home, when to sleep, when to eat, whom to be with, when to work and when to play for the last several months or years. Take that into consideration when you negotiate rules for living at home during vacations. Try to make rules that further your child's growth. Set standards that will move both of you forward toward interdependence rather than backward to dependence.

A client told me recently how much he hates to go home for vacation. Although he is a junior in college and has done very well, all the old high-school rules apply when he is home. He has a midnight curfew on Friday night, 11:00 p.m. on other nights. His father has called his girlfriend's house to be sure her parents are home if he is there with her. He has the same restrictions as his sisters who are in high school. "Doesn't he know I've been coming and going wherever I want for years?" this young man asks. The lack of respect he senses is driving him away. He takes every opportunity available to not go home.

Do not give your opinion unless you are asked. Keep in mind the developmental issues when you talk with your young adult children. In a conversation with a peer, there would be give and take, ideas flowing back and forth between you. There are times when that cannot seem to happen between child and parent; when you really need to not offer an opinion unless you are asked to do so. It took me a while to learn this, and most likely my children would say I have not arrived yet.

When Aaron told me he was thinking of not going on the choir tour to Europe, I did well. I did not react but asked for more information in a way that helped him talk. He wasn't asking for my opinion, and I was able to remember that. Eventually he did ask, and then I was free to give an opinion without it being a source of conflict. He ended up weighing all the information he had and choosing to go on the trip, knowing it was his decision to make. However, when Karlie told me of her plans to go to Zaire, I too quickly offered an opinion that was not asked for. She didn't have time to express herself before I was telling her what I thought in an attempt to influence her.

That messed up the communication on that subject for several weeks. I am still learning. First I want to listen. Then, when asked, I want to be able to give a well-thought-out response.

Expect conflict. For many children conflict is a means of breaking away. It often does not mean more than that. Young adults are learning to be different. They are learning to be individuals with separate voices. Conflict is inevitable, but it does not have to be divisive. Presume that your child will have different opinions, different beliefs and different ways of expressing those beliefs. That is part of finding their separateness. It may not last. Give them time and a place to push away so that their coming back will be their own.

Let others have a positive influence. How often I have heard my children express an idea that I have told them all their life as if it were something they have never heard before. The desire is to say, "I've told you that a hundred times," but then the idea would not feel like it was theirs. Now is the time to let others influence them. Let their boss tell them to get to work on time, their instructor tell them they did not put enough work into their last project or their friends tell them that smoking is stupid. Let them go and pour out their soul to a friend at church and thank God for providing them with godly people of influence in their lives.

I am so thankful for the people in my children's lives who have been there to guide and direct them in times of need. When my daughter Sarah made use of my friend Kay's expertise in problem solving, I was so thankful that she felt comfortable to do that. Another friend asked if I was jealous. Certainly not; I was thankful that she felt she had a godly older friend to talk to when she did not want to talk with her parents. As a church community we rear these children together, and I praise God for providing many wise people to guide them.

Welcome their friends as often as you can. It is amazing to me how many people pass through Seattle in the summer. Seattle is not exactly central to too many places. Yet many times throughout the summer our children's friends drop in. Mostly they are here looking for a free place to stay and to see my children. I am then given the opportunity to meet these friends and to interact with them. Since our children have gone to school on the East Coast, I value this time with their friends. It helps me understand my children better and gives me an opportunity to show hospitality to people who are important to them. Do not let that opportunity pass you by.

Remember, what you see in your child is not the end of the story. We know that when our children are two years old, behaving like two-year-olds, this stage will pass. The same is true when they are twenty. This is a transition time, and many of the difficulties of this stage will pass. God is not done with them yet, any more than he is done with us. Do not jump to conclusions about your child. Think of young adulthood as transition, as a time of solidifying a self. The teaching you have given will most likely come through in the end. Keep praying and believing that what God began in them he will bring to completion.

Surviving the Holidays: Tips for Young Adults

Respond rather than react to comments from your parents. As young adults ourselves, most of us made a commitment to keep an open mind when we got older. None of us wanted to be like the narrow-minded people we knew when we were growing up. Somehow, however, many of us lost that commitment to ourselves. We do not mean to be narrow-minded. It just seems to happen to many of us. We have had years of directing you, giving input and setting limits. That is a tough habit to change. Give us a break if you can, and know that we do want your growth. Often we are reacting out of eighteen years of history. We can be slow to make the change. Try not to react to the slowness of our thinking or the minute steps we take in letting you go. Dialogue. Negotiate. Keep talking. Help us understand you. We will get it eventually.

As with most people, reaction makes us dig in our heels. When I make a comment that is met with a sneer, I tend to cling to it more forcefully than I mean to. Challenge me when that seems appropriate, but try hard to do it without reaction and disrespect.

Negotiate the rules rather than break them. Many of the family rules you grew up with will seem silly to you now that you have lived on your own for a while. It is time to negotiate a new standard for yourself when you are at home. The temptation will be to ignore the rules and do what you want, but that only causes conflict. Attempt to talk with your parents. Let them know the level of independence you have experienced and how that has affected you. Let them know you no longer need their direct intervention in many areas. If they refuse to negotiate, let it go for a while, and then come back to it a few weeks later. Let them know you are serious about asking for a change, but ask respectfully.

A young woman I worked with in therapy told me of her parents' forbidding her to go camping without an adult present while she was home on summer vacation. It seemed like a strange rule to her, since she and her friends had gone camping together over spring break when she was at school. However, that was the rule for the home, and she was to abide by it. After bringing up the subject on two different occasions that ended in huge fights, she felt defeated.

Several weeks later she was able to approach her parents rationally, adult to adult, and heard their fears about her camping with friends. They were able to negotiate for a camping experience that her parents could tolerate. She agreed to go to a national park and to do so for only a weekend. Her parents felt that was safe enough, and it was something they could live with. It was not what she'd had in mind initially, but she too felt it was a good compromise. Once that was accomplished and her parents felt respected in the process, the rule fell away. The following summer, camping was no longer an issue. Her parents had let go enough to allow her to make her own decision in that area.

Realize that double messages are difficult to grasp. Most young adults are saying two things at the same time. On one hand you are saying "Let me go" and on the other "Keep my place." Parents will get confused if this is not talked about. At one point they will hear "let me go" and will do it. They might do something extreme, like renting out your room, or something not as extreme, like planning a trip without you. They may hear "keep my place" and volunteer you for a job at church or assign you chores without negotiating.

You want both things, of course, and so do your parents. Again, talking will help. Let them know that one subject may be about letting go and another about maintaining a place. You may need to tell them that you want to volunteer for your own jobs from now on. That may feel like a decision that is important for you to make for yourself. Another time you may want to be included in an event, and they will need to know that as well. Often I have to ask my children whether they will be joining us in an event. I cannot get it straight when they will and when they are wanting independence. But knowing I can ask helps. Let them know you want to be asked and also that you appreciate being thought of. Both things are true for now. That is what this time is all about.

Talk and talk some more. A gift you can give your parents is to let them know you during this time of your life. Sharing with them your victories and struggles will be a great gift to them. Often this will cause conflict, as your parents resist letting you have your own beliefs, thoughts and feelings. Yet it is so much better than silence.

Let them know what is important to you, what you are learning, who your friends are and what you are hoping for. This sharing will carry a lot of weight when it comes to negotiating in areas that are important to you. They will have a better sense of knowing who you are, with your own uniqueness. It will help to emphasize your differentness and not make it so scary to your parents. And they will feel connected to you. That connectedness will make letting go less frightening.

Remember, what you see in your parents is not the end of the story. Parents change too. As we survive letting go and still feel connected, we are more able to make further needed changes for our mutual growth. This is all new to us, and most people have a hard time learning new skills.

You may find that we do better with each child that comes along. The firstborn is the one we practiced on; we learn a little more through the secondborn and then have it down by the time the third one is going through it. Most of us are moving as fast as we can. The conflictual relationship that we seem to have with you now is a phase for us as well. God is not done with us yet. Please do not jump to conclusions about who we are or who we have become. Keep praying and trusting God to lead us to this new way of being that honors God and respects us both.

Remaining Friends

I write this one week before my second child's college graduation, three months before the third child leaves for college, while the oldest child supports himself in his career. I am feeling enormously blessed to have my adult children as friends, having survived so much of the transitional conflict from earlier years. We have all grown in the process of learning to see the world from another's perspective. Learning to negotiate and coming to believe we want what is best for all of us puts us on the same team. It is a great feeling!

While this is an important period of transition for ourselves and our adult children, our work is not yet done. We are needed to hold down the home fort, to be the rock of stability in times of need, to be available when they get off track and need to find a way back. During this transition they may take a number of goings and comings before they are gone for good.

The time of transition is a perfect opportunity for this. As our kids come and go on holidays or during summer breaks, they will have opportunities to push against us in ways that help establish an independent self. While this may not feel too comfortable to us at times, it's a great service we do our children. In this kicking they find a more solid self. If we can endure the challenges to our lifestyle, our beliefs, our theology and our habits, we will see our children growing into themselves. We hope that self will reflect the image of Christ that we hope for ourselves. Together we will be looking to God's Spirit to mold us, making us more like Christ and the interdependence of his church.

Exercise

Determine what tips work best for your family. Negotiate these guidelines with your children so you are working in harmony during visits home.

6

Family Gymnastics
Patterns, Roles & Triangles

....

Most of us are familiar with the overall design of our particular family interactions. Roles, patterns and triangles are a regular part of our family gymnastics. There are roles, or ways of behaving, that seem set for each member of the family. Other behaviors are so predictable they seem to be cut from a pattern. And there are ways of communicating between people that draw fairly clear guidelines about how talk flows in a family. These triangles dictate who talks about whom and where the alliances are in the family. When the adult child leaves home, these routines are tested. In reaction to the loss parents feel at this time, there is often a persistent pull by parents to keep everyone in his or her assigned place. This only contributes to the havoc in the family. Things are bound to change at this point.

The family is a network of patterns, roles and triangles that form a mosaic of connections and interconnections. In chapter five, noting how the family works hard to maintain stability in the midst of change, we referred to the well-choreographed dance between parents and siblings. New moves are learned in order to stay sufficiently balanced and to keep from stumbling. Learning new patterns of relating is both a challenge and an art.

If a family is able to make the necessary adjustments after a member leaves home, things will go quite smoothly. If not, there will be a strong temptation to seduce the person back into the customary routines. And if the family is successful in wooing that member back, he or she will be expected to play out a particular part in the old ways of relating. A typical unspoken message that keeps things from changing is "It is all right to leave home, but it is not all right to change your role in our well-established patterns." For example, a parent may call an adult child on the phone to talk about problems in the marriage in order to keep the child in the center of the parental marital conflict.

The questions for parents are, How do we become aware of our particular family gymnastics so we break free of their hold on us? How can we let go of our children's part in our marital fights? How can the family rearrange itself so everyone learns a more productive way of relating? These are some of the questions we hope to answer in this chapter.

Roles That Triangle

The psychological world has recognized the tendency of family members to play certain roles in their relationships. Most often we do this without giving much thought to what we are doing. Sometimes the roles are helpful. When an adult automatically comforts a hurt child, regardless of whether he or she knows the child, that can be a helpful experience for the one hurting. When a man or a woman answers a scream for help by attempting to rescue the one in danger, that is a courageous act for which we are all thankful. However, when we find ourselves repeatedly rescuing someone who does not need our help or calling for help when we are capable of meeting our own needs, we have fallen into unhealthy patterns that hinder growth. Let's look at some of the more obvious roles played by various family members in most homes.

The victim. Both parents and children can easily play the victim role. We do this when we see ourselves as helpless and at the mercy of others who can make or break our lives. We see others as more capable, getting better breaks and having more resources to succeed where we fail. We see our lives as being under the control of other people who determine our future. We think of ourselves as victims to the whims of others.

We do this as parents when we refuse to adjust to children having their own lives. We moan and groan and wait for them to visit so we can have a few minutes of happiness. When a child makes a decision we do not like, we cry out, "Look what you have done to me" in hopes that they will change their mind. Our happiness depends on their behavior toward us. We are victims to their will and decisions and dependent on them for our well-being.

Our children do a similar thing when they see themselves in a helpless state. The world is a tough place in which they have to survive. Sometimes taking on the role that says "I can't make it on my own. No one will let me succeed" seems easier than struggling to make our own way. The feeling that I am incompetent and everyone else is better than me is the victim role. When we feel that everyone is out to get us, no one appreciates us or we can never make it on our own, we are taking the victim stance.

When Brandon graduated from high school, he was ambivalent about what he should do with his life. He haphazardly applied to colleges, never putting in enough effort to write a thoughtful essay about his goals and future plans. He felt jealous when many of his friends got accepted and blamed his rejections on biases of admissions committees. He argued that his high-school grades should not matter and found excuses why his SAT scores were not high enough. He ended up delivering pizzas, complaining that he did not get paid enough for a job he hated.

Such a role is obviously debilitating. It can be an unending cycle of pessimism and failure for parents and children. And it is contrary to our faith. The victim role cannot coexist with belief in a God who is involved in our lives. We have an empowering God who enables us to reach our potential. We put this knowledge of God aside when we put on the victim role; the two do not mesh together.

The rescuer. Seeing the victim unable to function in the world he or she has created, the rescuer rushes to help. A rescuer comes with ideas, solutions and behaviors meant to save the victim from despair and to make him or her eternally thankful for the wisdom and care of the rescuer. The rescuer knows what needs to be done and is eager to communicate that knowledge. Parents who are rescuers take charge of their children, doing things for them they could and probably should do for themselves.

Kevin was being a rescuer when he filled out his daughter Alison's college applications for her. Alison was not getting to it, and Kevin wanted the applications done and done well. He spent all day working on three different applications and getting all the required documents together. Alison was glad they were done but not as thankful as Kevin thought she should be. But then, she had often taken it for granted when he did her homework for her also. Finally in late spring Alison settled on a college, and she went to school later that fall.

By the following spring it was clear to all that Alison was not going to make it. She had recruited a few short-term boyfriends to rescue her from various difficulties at college, but she was not surviving without her father to help her through. Alison flunked out by the end of her freshman year and was back home. Kevin had cemented his role as rescuer in Alison's life. In doing this he furthered her dependence on him; she was not encouraged to use or develop her own skills.

Our children come to our aid in a variety of ways as well. When we play the helpless victim, our children can rescue us by doing the very thing we want. When they change their plans and do not leave home, when they give up their dream and enter the family business instead, when they become who we want them to be rather than who they are, they come to rescue us in our victim role.

The persecutor. It can be frustrating to attempt to rescue victims who refuse to be rescued. We make wonderful suggestions on how their lives can be improved, and they ignore us. Something is always wrong with our suggestions, and the victim continues in the role. As our rescuing attempts fail, we begin to get angry. As the victim refuses to be helped, the rescuer turns to persecute. At other times it is the victim who moves to a new role. As the rescuer quits fixing things, the victim gets angry, persecuting the person who was the rescuer. Observe how this works in the following examples.

Kevin was furious with Alison when she flunked out of school. Even though it sounded like a cliché, he could not help but shout, "After all I did for you to get you through school and into college! How could you do this to me?" Kevin was very angry at first (persecutor), taking her actions personally, but eventually he began to make plans for what he thought Alison should do next (back to rescuing).

Shelly and John were concerned about their daughter's not having a job. Lina had been on her own for two years before she moved home again, and they were so glad to have her back. The plan was for Lina to stay with her parents and get back on her feet financially. But after seven months Lina had still not found work, and Shelly and John were frustrated.

They had tried their best to help. Shelly knew Lina was depressed when she first moved in with them, so she did not expect much from Lina. She was glad to have Lina under her care again and was happy to do things for her. Lina would sleep late in the mornings and stay out late at night. John found it irritating, but both parents wanted to help Lina. They offered to help Lina retrain herself and brought her brochures on various programs. They set up appointments with people they knew who might be helpful, but Lina rarely made it to the appointments.

Life was too hard for Lina. She was a failure. Why couldn't her parents see it and leave her alone? Nothing they suggested would work. Didn't they see that? Life was hard these days. It's not like it was when they were young. She certainly couldn't go out there and get a job. They don't pay anything these days. She wished her parents would get off her back and understand the situation.

As the months passed, Lina's parents changed from rescuers to persecutors. When they came home from work to see Lina still in bed, they screamed at her. John, who was normally a soft-spoken man, found himself calling Lina stupid and lazy and resenting the intrusion on his life. Lina became the butt of jokes around the house, and before long no one expected her to ever make it on her own.

As Shelly and John fell into their own victim roles with Lina, she began her persecution. "It's your fault nothing works for me!" she cried. Her accusations—no one ever helps me, no one is there for me, you made me come home, I didn't ask to be born—tore at her parents. Their friends felt sorry for Shelly and John and encouraged them to take a firmer stand with Lina, but they knew they could never do that.

Victim, rescuer, persecutor. The cycle goes round and round again. The roles change, the parts are shared, and the players stay stuck indefinitely. Surely there is an alternative to these roles.

Once such roles are set in stone, they are very difficult to change. Out of discomfort, however, parents gain the incentive to do something different. The immediate challenge is to figure out how to step out of the vicious cycle. For a start parents can formally acknowledge the part they play in the proverbial cycle. Then they can determine to step out of that role no matter how chaotic things get. As the old adage goes, we cannot change another person, but we can change ourselves. And in the process of changing yourself there will be an automatic change in the other two roles. If you stop rescuing, it does not pay off for a victim to stay in the victim role. When you let go of your persecutor role, the victim has to figure out what is wrong on his or her own. If you are no longer a victim, others cannot rescue you. It sounds rather simple, but it is very difficult to do. You can easily be drawn back in, but if you are persistent, you can break the cycle.

Empowering parents do not let themselves get caught in these roles. They work out their own marital relationship without asking their kids to play the rescuer role. They speak for themselves and know how to get their needs met through inner and external sources without putting themselves in the victim role. They face their own limitations forthrightly without needing anyone else to play the role of persecutor. They believe their adult children can find ways to meet their own needs without needing to rescue them. They do not have a need to persecute their children to get them to do something, for they need to persecute their children to get them to do something, for they let their children face the consequences of their own behavior. They assume their children will let their needs be known without having to be a victim, and they make decisions according to empowering principles. They stay interested in their adult children, giving advice when it is sought and responding to them as they would their adult friends. They allow their adult children to be adults.

Troublesome Threesomes

Having looked at the roles we play in the victim-rescuer-persecutor triangle, we turn to some other troublesome threesomes that can trap us in dysfunctional family interactions. How many of us have felt the experience of a parent standing between us and another or felt caught between our mother and our father? Or maybe you have felt a parent, often the father, to be so removed from the family that a coalition is formed with the mother. This circumstance later brings about the demise of the child-father relationship.

In the novel *My Name Is Asher Lev* author Chaim Potok lets us in on such a struggle a young Jewish boy has in his family threesome. In this moving story Asher, an artist, is able to express on canvas the pain he feels about how his mother was put in a difficult position between her son and her husband. She tried to protect them from each other without realizing the destructive effect it would have on all three. Asher proceeds to paint a crucifixion scene of his mother at the upstairs window of their home. There she stands, arms extended and wrists tied to the cords of the venetian blinds, against the cross of the windowpane. Father is on her right, dressed in hat and coat with attaché case in his hand, and Asher on her left, dressed in paint-splattered clothes and holding palette and paintbrush.

Later he explains the significance of this painting:

I split my mother's head into balanced segments, one looking at me, one looking at father and one looking upward. The torment, the tearing anguish I felt in her, I put into her mouth, into the twisting curve of her head, the arching of her slight body, the clenching of her small fists, the taut downward pointing of her thin legs. . . . For all the pain you suffered, my mama. For all the torment of your past and future years, my mama. For all the anguish this picture of pain will cause you. For the unspeakable mystery that brings good fathers and sons into the world and lets a mother watch them tear at each other's throats. For the Master of the Universe, whose suffering world I do not comprehend. (Potok 1972:312-13) Here an observant Jew uses the image of crucifixion as a way to depict the anguish of a family triangle.

Freedom to be a great artist came to Asher Lev at an enormous price. His mother's good intentions kept the father and son from working out their differences. Since all communication went through her, they had limited opportunity to become intimate with each other. Without her standing in that place, Asher and his father might have been able to face each other directly and find the healing they needed. Instead of creating a bridge, she became a barrier to intimacy between them.

We do that as parents when we believe that we can handle something our child is doing or going through better than our spouse can. By directing a child to communicate through us or intercepting communication between our spouse and child, we perpetuate a triangle. While we appear to be the good guy to our child, we paint the other parent as weak or an outsider.

Sylvia grew up with a volatile father who had little control over his anger. After she married mellow John, she often acted as if his temper were volatile as well. When their son, Paul, scratched the car, Sylvia attempted to keep the information from John. When Paul was doing poorly in high-school math, Sylvia decided it would be best for Paul not to let his father know. When Paul needed something from his father, he learned it was best to ask his mother to get the information for him. They established a clear triangle for communication between Paul and John. John began to believe that he could not talk to his son. Letting Sylvia handle things was easy, and soon he was asking her what Paul thought and felt about things, making the triangle an even stronger one.

When it was time for Paul to leave home, Sylvia was in anguish. She did everything to keep him from leaving. She feigned illness that kept him home for several months. She laid a guilt trip on him for leaving. John stayed out of the picture. He was so used to not being involved with Paul firsthand that it never occurred to him to help now. Finally Paul broke free, with much turmoil and pain for all. From a place of distance, however, the family began to heal their relationships.

Sylvia started learning to relate to John without Paul as a buffer. John began a direct relationship with his son, made possible by Paul's phone conversations to him, which did not involve Sylvia. Relationships began to improve all around as direct communication began to take place. Even Sylvia and John began to talk directly to each other and felt the effects of deepened intimacy.

A similar thing happened to Asher Lev. Leaving home finally changed that rigid threesome pattern and opened the way for personal growth and renewed closeness between his parents. At the end of the novel we hear Asher talk about what happened after he left home:

> They had lived years without me. Now they possessed a language of shared experience in which I was nonexistent. Often they would slip into the shorthand of private signs and notations that form the speech of people who have been together intimately for great lengths of time. There were smiles, expressions . . . grimaces . . . quiet laughter. It sounded strange to hear them laughing about my mother's habit of waiting at windows. They talked to each other with ease and assurance and knowing intimacy. Often I felt they were together now as they had been before I was born. . . . My father's attitude to my work had undergone a quiet change. He lived now upon a mountain of achievement that gave him the strength to be indifferent about my art and no longer to see it as a threat. He regarded me as if from a distance and disliked me without rage. (Potok 1972:277-78)

While things still were not perfect between them as father and son, now they would have the potential to work out a more satisfying relationship.

The Go-Between Pattern
Forming coalitions in which two people stand against the third is

another destructive pattern of relating. Often when this is happening in the family it is particularly difficult for the young adult to leave home successfully. Standing as a go-between in any relationship is a heavy burden. While there are many possible scenarios of this triangle, a breakdown in relationships is inevitable.

In some families one parent takes on the designated go-between role. A typical scenario is when Mother becomes the communication broker. Her children nearly always ask her permission when needed, let her know things they need, tell her when they need to get a message to Dad or even how they feel about their father. She is the hub of the wheel when it comes to family interactions, whether the communication is coming from Dad ("Tell those kids to be home on time") or from the children to the father ("Tell Dad to let me have the car"). This mother is busy being the go-between, and the children and father never develop a relationship with each other.

Sometimes a family member takes on this role as peacekeeper of the family. This member sees himself or herself as the problem solver in the family. This person may have an aversion to conflict and may intervene between family members to maintain peace at all costs. This situation may be due to a parent's absence (business, travel, service professional, military deployment), which leads children naturally to lean on the parent at home.

In father-absent homes mothers tend to establish close ties with their children. This is not a bad thing in itself, but when children are alienated from their father and/or sense their mother is overly dependent on them, they may have trouble leaving her. Often much of her life is centered on rearing children, and it can be quite a blow when her children leave and no one is there to fill the void.

The same thing can occur in two-parent homes when either parent looks to the children to meet emotional needs because he or she feels neglected by the spouse. In this case children are saddled with the responsibility to care for a depressed, dejected or lonely parent. The distant spouse plunges further into whatever takes him or her away from the family. The pattern repeats itself like a memorized paragraph in the family story.

A son or daughter may become a substitute spouse, friend or confidant to the mother or father. In this caretaking role the child feels more than responsible for the well-being of the parent. When it is time to venture out to find an identity, it's nearly impossible for the child to leave. "Who will keep the family going when I'm gone?" is the nagging question in this person's mind.

A natural occurrence of this pattern is seen in a military family where deployment—whether it is routine leaves or a call to active duty during a war—regularly removes one parent from the home. The film *The Great Santini* depicts what it is like for Ben, the eighteen-year-old son of a marine captain, who tries to separate himself from his role as family protector in his father's absence. The mission canot be argued. After all, his father, Bull Meechum, has a responsibility to his country as the greatest fighter pilot of all. Bull loves his career but loses the love and respect of his family as a result of his choice to remain distant from them. Unable to make a significant connection with his father, Ben is unable to find himself or to know where he is headed in life.

In search for his identity Ben listens to his mother, who has been the dominant parent for eighteen years, as she tells him that gentleness is what she most admires in a man. His father, however, wakes him up at 4:00 a.m. to give him his old flight jacket as a birthday present. He's been waiting for this occasion since the day Ben was born, he announces. Ben desperately wants to connect with his father, and as he goes through the ritual of putting on that leather jacket, his father tells the story about the day he was born.

It is a wonderful opportunity for them to connect, it is a rite of passage for Ben, and yet an obligation goes along with it. Being a real man means he must register for the draft and follow in his father's footsteps. This tears into the heart of Ben, who has dreamed of becoming a writer. In the turmoil of these mixed messages Ben struggles with how he can find approval from his father and yet pursue his dreams that take him in another direction. No wonder he cannot find a way to leave home and become his own person.

And Ben struggles with yet another issue. He has become his mother's protector and confidant. His siblings look to him, as the eldest sibling, for leadership in the home. Ben does not know what to do with the anger he feels toward his father when he is abusive to his mother and when his drinking disrupts the family. It is better when he is off to war, Ben states, because then he can fight someone his own size.

This model of manhood leaves much to be desired. The family relationships are also complicated because Ben cannot grasp the deep resentment his father feels toward him because of the intimate relationship he shares with his mother. Under these circumstances leaving home is seen as an unachievable goal. Finding his way into adulthood has been circumvented by persistent family patterns that Ben is not able to escape on his own.

Problematic Patterns

"I've had so many homes and left these homes so many times that the idea of leaving home has very little meaning to me. It's a twisted way to live, and it twists up your life." This statement by a disillusioned young woman from a parent-absent home rings true for many young people. Parents who put their work above their family often reap trouble for their children. The child is required to make adjustments in order to accommodate a parent's career or cope with that absent parent. This can lead to different configurations in the family dynamics.

In many cases the stay-at-home parent is exceptionally capable and takes on the leadership of the family without unduly relying on her or his children. But when the responsibility is too much for the parent, the children inevitably take on parenting responsibility. The reaction can be intense anger, because these children feel they have been abandoned by both parents.

Putting one's career ahead of the family, having to leave on a moment's notice, has unique ramifications for many adult children. Expectations about keeping the home fires burning or being in charge while the father or mother is gone may also limit a young person's freedom to leave home when it is time. Because their parents depend on them to keep the family intact, the adult children will be reluctant to leave.

Similar dynamics are evident in families who experience the premature leaving of a parent through death, disease, divorce or desertion. Children in these homes must pull together to make up for that loss. It is a frightening experience for a child to be left behind by a parent, no matter what the age or the circumstance of the leaving.

Devastated by such a situation, Winston drew a picture of himself, his mother and his sister standing outside their front door looking forlorn and confused, gazing into the dark skies for answers. He commented, "I never left home! It was my father who left us, and I have not seen him since that day he walked out. I became a father to my little sister and a substitute husband to my mother. Mother leaned on me for advice, and my little sister leaned on me for love. I felt I had to be tough and strong to make up for his cowardly behavior."

We can hear the depth of the hurt and anger in Winston, who at twenty-five cannot conceive of leaving his mother and sister in order to pursue his life dreams. Even if he wants to go, he can't find enough of himself to consider a life of his own.

Sometimes the idea of leaving home takes this strange turn because the parents have left their children prematurely. Whether it is a job-related absence or unforeseen circumstances, this is always a difficult experience. One young woman talked about the day her mother left home, never to return. Stunned by her action, the family did the only thing they could do: tried to survive without her. Being the oldest, this young woman took on responsibility for her younger siblings. Her father leaned on her for comfort as he tried to make sense of why his wife left or when he felt humiliated by trying to explain her actions to others. It was not long till he became seriously depressed and ended his life.

His suicide added to the heartache. Janice and her brothers and sisters were split up among relatives and grew up without the secure love and guidance of their parents. Such sacrifices in childhood take a huge toll on one's future. It is hard to move forward in life when such harsh realities knock your very breath away.

When a parent lacks self-esteem and falls apart after a spouse is gone, he or she may escape through depression, physical illness, alcoholism or other addictions. In this situation the kids often end up parenting their parents. Adolescent males seem to struggle even more when they live with a single mother in that situation. Showing more aggressive and antisocial behavior, they are hard to handle. While girls adjust more rapidly initially, they may suffer from depression or lowered self-esteem later. A son or a daughter sometimes finds it difficult to leave the single parent, who has become extremely dependent. Or when the child leaves it may be in a gruff manner, perhaps to show an immunity to the emotional connection.

When the leaving-home person has served as the caretaker, siblings may also freak out, fearing they will be unable to live up to the responsibility. "Will Mom get depressed or Father have another affair when I take over?" The pressure is too much for them to bear. Therefore younger siblings may take drastic measures (acting-in or acting-out behaviors) in order to get an older sibling back into the home.

Whenever a child attempts to take on a parent's role, it is problematic. In a single-parent home, the support of an extended family or friendship network can provide needed resources so adult children can move ahead with their lives without feeling guilty for leaving the parent. It is natural for a single parent to depend more on children for emotional support. But this pattern becomes detrimental when the child gets trapped into the caretaking role. As long as a single parent maintains other adult relationships, the child will not feel obligated to stay to take care of the family. Only when children are free of such family triangles will they be able to separate and develop lives of their own.

When both parents are busy with their careers or jobs, children can feel just as neglected and emotionally unprepared to leave home. While we agree that many dual-earner parents, single parents and stepparents do an amazing job of developing secure, well-adjusted and independent children who experience a smooth leave-taking, there are also homes in which instability is predictable. The overfunctioning of either a parent or a child must be protested. The overinvolved mother and underinvolved father is a common problematic pattern that must be avoided. The only way to break this disruptive pattern is for parents to work out their relationship without triangling in the children. In addition, both parents must take on their rightful responsibility for involvement in their children's lives.

Breaking Old Patterns and Creating New Ways

However our children are changed by the leaving-home experience, they will inevitably feel an uncanny tendency to do the old dance when they step inside the front door. Jennifer remarks, "I hate the way I behave when I'm back home. I don't know what comes over me. I've been on my own for the past four years, but when I come home I'm a little kid again. There is a powerful pull to go back to the old ways of relating. It's like my mature self recedes into the background and my angry little girl returns. I lose my vitality as an independent person and go back to my childish ways."

The idea of gaining a separate sense of self means a young person is able to come back into the family without getting caught in those old family roles and patterns. When one is differentiated from the family of origin, it is no longer enticing to join in the familiar family gymnastics. Young people have learned to flex their own muscles, establish their own routines and accomplish their unique goals. And while the young adult has been gone, their parents and other family members have developed movements of their own. The family itself has made sufficient changes.

Once adult children return home, it is best for them to sit on the sidelines for a while before entering back in.They must finesse their way in, and as they do, they must contribute some unique moves of their own. If the family makes it impossible for them to reenter, this can also be a dilemma. Fearful of being left out, some adult children will storm back in to regain their old place. Or, fearful of being abandoned by their children, parents will develop schemes to get them back home.

However, once sons or daughters are able to acknowledge the compelling pull of the old family patterns, they have a chance to do something intentionally different to change them. Once parents recognize the patterns, they also have the opportunity to make the appropriate adjustments. Change is not easy, but it is exciting, for it brings about the possibility of new choices that can propel the entire family forward. Parents who successfully develop advanced moves in the absence of their adult children will welcome adult children back to the family with new status. If it has been impossible to make adjustments, parents may resort to making such a clean break that there is no room for returning adult children. Or they may attempt to keep everything the same so returning adult children take up their old roles and patterns.

Differentiation from one's family of origin not only brings objectivity but also gives the capacity to resist the family pull. By stepping back we can take the role of a knowing observer who refuses to get hooked by the old patterns. Rather than reacting in predictable ways of the past, parents and adult children can find alternative ways that work for them. The leaving-home juncture compels a family to ask important questions about interaction patterns and prescribed roles.

This offers an opportunity for parents and adult children to talk together about the discomfort they feel when children come home for a visit. Asking each other questions about what roles are played and why that role was assigned to a particular family member can prove enlightening. Viewing family gymnastics from multiple points of view provides a fresh outlook. Through mutual dialogue, the family can openly discuss together how each one feels about the roles and work together to make changes. Once the patterns and roles are recognized, they can be anticipated and resisted so that new patterns and roles can be put into place.

Becoming independent means that our children get beyond a narrow self-focus, expanding their capacity for greater commitment, empathy and care for others. An ability to take in the needs of others is what covenant is essentially about. Mutual covenant between parent and child changes from a one-way, dependent relationship to a more equal and mutual one. It offers a chance to renew our relationship with our adult children, relating on an adult-to-adult level and adding a warmth and fullness to our lives. The complete leaving-home proc-

The final performance, however, comes through mutual respect and appropriate timing, so that positive changes have made an even more beautiful mosaic.

A New View of Things

Rodney Clapp makes this observation: "When family is not the whole world, parents can let children go and in turn find themselves reclaimed as parents. Truly letting a child go is hard, not only because of the pain of separation, but because a child fully released will reclaim and reshape the relationship in a way that may not be entirely to the parents' liking. This will especially be the case where the wounds and bruises of childhood are deep. In those situations some parents will want to insist that the past is done and gone, to imagine a sentimental and idyllic childhood" (Clapp 1993:86).

As parents release their hold on children, they are finally free to return and develop a relationship with their parents that indeed changes parents as well. We have come full cycle as they reclaim us and we reclaim the new selves we have become. Their way of interacting with us reflects the adults they have become. We grow into a new relationship that reflects the changes we have made together.

Children who leave have now had life experiences apart from us that give them the opportunity to see us and the patterns of our family from a new vantage point. The separation makes it possible for them to question their roles and their part in the routines. This new perspective helps them reenter the game and perform some intriguing new moves of their own. They may invite their parents to join them in some unfamiliar acrobatics. This is a chance for creative growth. Getting away has given them a new view of us. In rearranging ourselves as a family without them, we too can take a fresh look at the new moves and make some important revisions. We may have been able to sidestep some of the ineffective patterns and eliminate some of the disharmony.

When adult children mature, they often have a more sympathetic understanding of their parents. Having more empathy for what it takes to be in relationship or rear a family of their own, they can take a deeper view of individual members as well as the interactions between them. From this vantage point they can recognize the wounds, hurts and deficits that have come from their parents' families of origin. For example, a grown daughter begins to understand why her mother held on so tightly to her power or why her father is unable to express his feelings. The blinders come off through life experiences during our time away from home.

How vividly I (Judy) remember the day I viewed my dad through different eyes. I had seen him as a bitter, pessimistic, selfish man most of my life. But as an adult my eyes were opened as I began to hear the story of how he had been rejected by an uncaring, self-serving father. Insight about the agony of his harshly critical and demeaning childhood experience led to understanding and compassion. This new view of him in the context of his family of origin helped me realize that he could not love me very well because he was never loved himself. Coming to grips with your own pain by acknowledging the pain of your parents brings a new view of things that heals.

Sometimes the road is long and the relationship suffers for lack of healing between members. It is possible that by the time members are able to deal with the problems between them, drastic changes have already occurred. This was true for Godric, the saintly character in a Frederick Buechner novel. When he finally returned to his parents' house, his mother announced that his father was dead. Godric responded, "The sadness was I'd lost a father I had never fully found. It's like a tune that ends before you've heard it out. Your whole life through you search to catch the strain, and seek the face you've lost in strangers' faces" (Buechner 1980:51). Later he rethinks his role in the relationship. "Dear Christ, have mercy on my soul. . . . I have chided you for failing as a father, too spent from grubbing to have any love to spend on me. Maybe it was the other way around, and it was I that failed you as a son. Did I ever bring you broth? Was any word I ever spoke a word to cheer your weariness?" (Buechner 1980:103).

Many of us, like Godric, hope we can reconcile someday and establish a renewed relationship as parents and adult children. With failures acknowledged on both parts, growth is inevitable. Leaving failures acknowledged on both parts, growth is inevitable. Leaving home can be an occasion for celebration and growth for all.

Looking back at our families once we have left can bring new growth in many ways. This can be an opportunity to view from a distance what we could not see up close. Getting a perspective on our failures and the difficulties in the relationships within our families has the potential to transform us. From this distance we can more clearly see our part and make significant changes in behavior. Being able to leave the situation and go to our own place gives additional courage to bring up the issues that involve our family and to attempt to work them through together. Many young people use this time to enter therapy and attempt to resolve unfinished business from their family of origin that disables them in some way. It is a good time to work through losses and other pain before it impacts life any further.

As parents we can be helpful here. This time can be greatly enhanced by our ability to own our mistakes and to hear what our children are working through. If we are fortunate enough to have children who are willing to communicate with us as they work on past issues, we can be a part of their healing (see Balswick and Piper 1995).

Exercise
Think about the roles you play with your adult child. Do these roles limit your child's life and future? Are you remaining in old roles or patterns, or are you developing new ways of relating? The following questions will help you evaluate yourself.

☐ Does you child feel obligated to make your life happy?

☐ Are you taking a go-between role in any relationships?

☐ Does your behavior reflect a belief in your children that encourages independence?

☐ How is God at work in your relationships with your adult children?

Commit yourself to relating in new ways and seeing your children as the adults they hope to become.

7

Dealing with Differences

....

We cannot anticipate how the choices our children make will affect our lives, but they do. Each decision they make has potential for great happiness or great sadness, for them and often for us. Sometimes we will feel a bitter disappointment; at other times we revel in the successes of their life choices. No matter how old they are, parents are vulnerable and can be shattered by unfortunate or even tragic choices. In this chapter and the next we will consider how we can respond to our children's choices in empowering ways. We will also consider choices that have the potential to rupture our relationships and how we can remain faithful through the hard times.

You are aware of the familiar teaching that our children belong to God and are loaned to us for a time. We are to care for them, encourage them and teach them of their Savior, Jesus. And as they come to know Christ and to know themselves in relation to God, they get a sense of their own call. As they begin to live out this call, they develop a lifestyle that we may or may not encourage. Yet as Christians we know we are not to be raising clones of ourselves but images of Christ.

Some children reject the call of Christ on their lives. Perhaps this is the most painful experience parents must grasp. And yet here too our response must be one that honors God and maintains a positive relationship with our child, providing a way back to Christ should he or she choose to return.

Families respond differently to various lifestyle choices. In some families it is okay to leave, but the rules around leaving and being an adult are specific, even if they are unspoken. Leaving home may be okay but moving to another state may not. Going to college may be okay, but living on campus may break a rule. Working in the business world may be acceptable but having your own business may not. Marrying may be encouraged, but marrying someone from a different denomination or culture may cause a problem.

How do we not only let our children go but also be accepting of the lives they lead? It is easy to think we know the best way to go about living life. We have been at it much longer and have so many good ideas to pass on to our children. But so often, just as when they were two years old, they want to do it themselves. And they want to do it their way.

If You Knew What I Know

It is natural to want to pass on all we can to our children. In talking with Micah recently I (Boni) realized how deeply this man loved his daughter. He wanted so much for her. He could agree that the man Hannah loved was a good guy, but he could not give his blessing on his daughter's marriage. Now it looked as if they were going to marry without his blessing. Micah agonized over the fact that they had no down payment for a house and would have to live in a little apartment. Hannah was going to have to work while Caleb finished graduate school. They would never get ahead at that rate. No, he could not bless such a thing.

In talking to Micah I learned that he'd had a meager beginning in his marriage. Life was hard then, and he did not want his daughter to go through the rough financial times that he and Christina had. As we talked he realized that what he wanted for Hannah was to begin her adult life in a financial situation similar to the one she was used to. As he stated that dream out loud, he saw the absurdity of it. Our children must begin at the beginning, and the way they go about that may be a legitimate route.

Could their way be right? Don't they want the wealth of advice we have to offer? Why would they not take joyfully the ease our experience could bring them? How can we know when we are being intrusive and when our adult children need our intervention or advice? How can we break dysfunctional patterns of interacting that bring both parents and young adults grief? These are some of the questions we hope to answer in this chapter.

Belief in Our Children

Kira was concerned about her son Jaime's choices in many areas. As her friend Kerry listened to her concerns, Kerry commented on how incompetent Jaime must be. Kira was taken aback. That was not the case at all. Jaime was a competent, talented young man. Yet until she heard herself through her friend's ears she had not realized the image she portrayed of her son. She wondered, "Is that the message I give him? Does he think I believe him to be incompetent?"

That opened up a new thought for Kira and a new way of relating to Jaime. Rather than giving him the message that he is not capable of succeeding, she began trying to communicate her belief in him as a competent adult. It was hard work at first. She was unaware of how often she undermined his competence. But she was determined to make the change and to communicate to her son the belief in him that she felt in her heart.

Do you realize how much you communicate without ever opening your mouth? I remember thinking that the hardest part of parenting adult children was keeping my mouth shut. It seemed a major life task to me. I believed strongly that I must pick my battles carefully, but that did not stop me from having opinions on nearly everything my children did. Keeping quiet was exhausting.

I thought I did a rather good job of it, however, until I talked to my children about it. It seems I still communicate what I am thinking. My body language says, "You were out too late last night," "I don't approve of that boyfriend," "I don't approve of your going to that church" or any number of thoughts I meant to keep hidden. In fact these were not the battles I wanted to fight. They were not events that I believed to be of crucial importance in my life or that of my child. But the message I often gave to my children is that they are not doing it my way, so they are not doing it right.

Having a judgmental attitude toward areas of life that God leaves to a person's discretion can be damaging for anyone to live under. When that person is a child who values the love and opinion of his or her parents, it is even more damaging.

Perhaps it comes back to trust once again. We have the wonderful opportunity of watching God at work in our children's lives. How God is going to open this flower of youth and bring it to completion may be completely different from how God works in us. To manipulate our children so that their paths match or avoid our own gives no acknowledgment of God's sovereignty in their lives.

Of course we know that some young adults are out of the will of God and are participating in behavior that we cannot condone. We will discuss our responses to that in the next chapter. The point here is that so much of what we worry about or criticize in our children has more to do with our will than God's will. We have a tendency to want to form our children in our image rather than giving them up to God to be transformed into the image of his Son.

The Gap Is Real

I remember the many discussions we would have with our daughter Sarah before she went out on a date. We would ask all the usual questions our parents asked us: "Where are you going? When do you expect to be home? Who will be there?" One question was different, however: "Which one of you is driving?" That was a question never asked when we were young: boys always did the driving. That is not the case anymore. Nor do boys do all the calling or arranging. Things have changed in that area.

Our son, Aaron, works as an accountant in Seattle. In our day that meant wearing a suit and tie to work. But Aaron wears jeans and T-shirts and still looks better than does his boss, who comes in sweats. Another change we must adjust to.

The generation gap needs to be recognized for what it is: a different way of looking at things. Our generation was not right when we wore bell bottoms any more than this one is wrong to wear combat boots. I (Judy) had trouble getting permission to pierce my ears because my mother thought it was worldly, whereas my son came home with a pierced ear without even asking me. It is God's way that must be held up as the model to follow, whether we are of this generation, the past or the future. Doing anything else gives a wrong message to the next generation. We cannot pretend that our preferences are anything other than what they are. Because one prefers the dainty female look does not make the yuppie look wrong. The clashes between personal preferences are not worth the ruin of a relationship. The clashes between values are another matter. A worthy moral cause is always worth the fight. In those cases we hope a way will be found to bridge the gap.

How Could You?

We have often sat with parents in therapy as they agonized over the pain their children were causing them. When a son moves in with his girlfriend, the response is often "How could he do this to me?" Or when a daughter does not visit as often as the parents might want, the parents can easily take it personally. We often expect that a behavior of another person is done against us rather than being something they decided to do for themselves.

There is an enormous difference between those two beliefs. When we take our child's choices as persecutions directed at us, we are personalizing their actions. We may or may not be accurate in doing that. Our daughter may not have considered us in the busyness of her life. Our son may believe he is old enough to make a choice about his living arrangements. It may be a decision based entirely on the adult child's own desires or needs. Considering our feelings may have been an afterthought, if that. When we tend to see ourselves in this reactive position, we are taking on a victim mentality (chapter six). That is one of the dysfunctional roles we want to leave behind, focusing instead on how we will be able to accept the differences between us in a way that preserves the relationship and does not compromise our beliefs.

My Life!
Conflicts about differing lifestyles seem to be common in most Western extended families. Our parents, who came out of the Depression, were shocked to see that many of us who grew up in the 1960s had no concern for the future and were excited to live for the moment. As we became parents, many of us were shocked to find ourselves rearing conservative children who work sixty-hour weeks and are willing to spend money on military defense. Perhaps these ideologies come and go in waves. Perhaps differing lifestyles are inevitable.

The challenge for us as believers is to find a Christian lifestyle to live and to encourage our children to do the same in their quest. God gives us enormous leeway. He values our differences and desires a unique life for each of us. And that is the model he demonstrates for us as we parent.

Sitting with a father and son in therapy, I (Boni) witnessed the agony of the fight for freedom that comes in some families. Tony was determined to live his own life. His father, Adam, wanted that too but did not approve of the choices Tony was making. With each concern Adam voiced, Tony repeated the same phrase: "Dad, it is my life." Adam was concerned about the amount of money Tony was making working for a mission. And what about the fact that Tony had no car, no life insurance, no stable place to live? Didn't Tony realize that other young men his age were starting careers, getting ahead and looking for a future? And the woman Tony was hanging around with was not a suitable match. Was he really expecting to bring her home to meet the family? "Dad, it is my life!"

That was all there was to say about it. It was the major message that Tony wanted Adam to hear. Tony wanted to live his own life. Adam had had his opportunity to live his own life. It was Tony's turn, and he longed for his father to acknowledge that.

When our children were young, we bought a small sailboat that we would take to the lakes in Seattle. We had many good years taking our turn out on the boat while others picnicked and swam offshore. We imagined sailing being a big part of our children's lives for years to come. However, when they got older, jet skis and power boats were what fascinated them. We shook our heads. *What is wrong with them? Everyone knows that sailboats are so much better—not to be dependent on fuel, avoiding all the noise of the motor. They cannot prefer all that to the wind in the sails!*

Does God say one is better than the other? Could it be a personal preference? Could it have to do with different lifestyle choices that reflect many, many different areas? Do they at some point get to choose? Which type of boat they enjoy. Which job they will take. Whom they will marry. How they will live. Boat choices are an insignificant matter. But demanding sameness can be debilitating whether it involves boats, a spouse, jobs, denominations or a variety of life choices God gives.

Choosing Battles

In previous chapters we have mentioned the importance of carefully selecting which battles to fight and which to ignore. Let us say a few more words about this issue. The stance that we continually want to have with our adult children is one that will move them toward the life tasks mentioned in chapter two. These are to develop autonomy, interpersonal relationships and purpose. But that is not enough. We also want a stance that encourages their individuation in Christ and an interdependence between them and other believers, including their parents.

Battles that are important enough to fight involve choices that do not support these concepts. For example, children who choose to use drugs are not making a choice that furthers them in their developmental tasks, furthers their individuation in Christ or supports an interdependence among friends. Nothing about that choice produces growth in a young adult. Yet there are parents who say at that point, "It is his life," and choose to ignore the fact that their son is doing drugs. They are refusing to fight a battle we believe is worth fighting.

Or think of the young adult who is abusing her body through laxatives and the binge/purge syndrome. Nothing about that behavior will strengthen the character or produce growth in that young woman. Yet many parents choose to ignore the problem, hoping it will go away.

What about when a young person chooses a vocation we do not approve of? Perhaps the daughter of a research scientist decides to work in a daycare center or the son of a pastor chooses to climb the corporate ladder. Each of these vocations can be followed while the children further their individuation in Christ and develop responsible relationships in a believing community. The tasks they are pursuing developmentally will not be affected by any of those career choices if their gifts are suited accordingly. To fight such a battle would hinder the growth of the young person in all three areas of growth. The best option in this case is to keep our opinions to ourselves and encourage our children as they seek God's will.

In another situation it may be that our adult child intends to marry a non-Christian, an act we know is contrary to God's will for believers. Their behavior may not affect them developmentally but may have enormous consequences, weakening their commitment to Christ or their desire to be part of a community of believers. They are about to take an action that will have consequences affecting the rest of their lives. To ignore their intent would be equally unhelpful. But what are you to do about it?

How to Do Battle

What does doing battle mean between a parent and a young adult child? When we think of the battles that are waged today as well as in times past, we think of blood and death. That is exactly what we do not want to happen in our relationships with our children. Our goal must always be to encourage our children toward God and thus toward personal growth. Screaming, fighting, hitting, permanent separation and other things that reflect a war between us are not the answer.

As adults we want to be treated with respect when we are challenged regarding our behavior or intentions. Our young adult children are no different. As we would with a friend we dearly love and are deeply concerned about, we need to plan a way of talking with our children that would be respectful and also show our love and concern for them.

Do we scream, "I found drugs in your pocket! You are grounded!" "I am going to force this food down your throat and you will never purge again. Do you hear me, young lady?" "You will go to hell if you marry her. Do you realize that?" These are not ways of talking to someone you respect or hope to encourage. Our delivery is important when we choose to confront a person about his or her behavior, regardless of whether that person is related to us.

The battle always has the purpose of showing love, demonstrating respect and creating a dialogue that may bring about change. Ultimately it is the decision of the young adult to change the behavior or not. We can no longer take the car away or ground them. What we can do is hope for discussion and an exchange that would be thought-provoking for both of us. We may come to understand them better as we talk, and they may come to know us more fully as well. If we are available to participate in this interchange with a desire for health and growth, we will each be blessed.

Doing Battle with Style

One way family members can approach their conflicts is to recognize that each member tends to have a different style in dealing with disagreements. It is as if our personalities and experiences mold us in unique ways to do what works best for us during a conflict. In this section we will describe five common styles that people naturally gravitate to when they are engaged in family fights. You will see that each style has strengths and weaknesses, and therefore no one style is right or wrong or superior. Any one of the styles has the potential to work well or cause havoc, so it behooves us to learn ways to work together so that we create solutions rather than diversions. When individual styles are complementary rather than disruptive, there will be a greater possibility of coming to mutually satisfying solutions.

A good way to begin is to look at the following descriptions of the various styles and identify the style you most commonly use in your family relationships. It goes without saying that each of us uses every one of the styles in different situations, but in this case we want you to honestly consider the first impulse you have when conflict arises in your home. This is your natural tendency, and you most likely learned your style growing up in your own family. The next step is to identify the style of other family members so you can more fully understand the breakdown that occurs during family conflicts. The goal is to recognize your different styles. Without judging others, you can determine what you need to do so your styles work for rather than against you.

Winner: You are verbally astute and particularly good at making a case for your side of any argument. You rather enjoy a good fight, for it gives you a chance to let the other person know all the reasons you are right. Your logical arguments are presented with ease and intensity, and you believe that if others would be rational enough to listen to your way of thinking, they would be sure you are correct. You enjoy it when others banter with you and express their opinions because it gives you a chance to strengthen your side of the argument. You are most likely considered a winner in life outside the family, and you may be in a position of authority in which you must act decisively.

You are adept at the art of persuasion, which is both your greatest strength and liability. When you win your family fights, you risk losing your relationships in the process of proving you are right. Your young adult children learn how to turn a deaf ear to your arguments. They know there is no way to persuade you, since you are so convinced of your position. Stan tolerated his father's strong opinions and then went out and did his own thing in secret. That was easier than trying to debate the issues when he knew he could never have an honest dialogue.

Yielder: You hold others in great regard and tend to give in to what they want in an argument. If you have a point of view, few know what it is, because you do not assert your ideas or desires during a fight. Servanthood and submission are highly valued because you believe they lead to peace and are the Christian way to respond to conflict. Being sensitive to the needs of others, you tend to put your own needs aside, and soon you are actually unaware of what you want or think when you are asked. Sometimes others take advantage of you, but if you feel angry about this you do not express anger openly. You may be able to let your wants be known through subtle, covert messages (sometimes referred to as passive-aggressive actions), but they are easily disregarded.

When a parent yields to an adult child, that child may feel superior and guilty at the same time. Knowing that they should not take advantage of a parent's sacrificial stance, they may secretly wish you would stand up for yourself and be a stronger parent. Jessie desperately wanted her mother to give her guidance when she started dating, but Sally's lack of opinion left her in the dark, fending for herself. Later she expressed anger toward Sally when she found herself in a difficult situation with her boyfriend.

Compromiser: You believe everyone, including yourself, should have a voice in the controversy because finding a compromise is best for everyone concerned. You know that everyone cannot be absolutely happy with any decision, so you are sure that if each one gives a little, they will also get a little of what they need in return. Negotiating family differences takes time. The democratic method (family council) is best for resolving conflicts because it is a place where everyone listens to the opinions of others. Being a realist rather than an idealist, you believe the best way to resolve family conflicts is to find a workable solution that everybody can live with. Even though you are willing to compromise for peace, you are not willing to compromise personal or religious values you hold dear.

At the same time you allow others to hold values that are different from your own without trying to persuade them of your position. Willing to forgo a personal desire for the good of the whole, sometimes you can be too flexible. It is conceivable that compromisers give in to their children too easily rather than working out a mutually satisfactory decision. Most compromisers will not relinquish their rightful leadership role but will go to great lengths to listen to and respect the ideas of their children before arriving at a final solution. Sometimes compromisers feel they never get exactly what they wanted in the first place. And when adult children are unwilling to compromise, the parent may revert to yielding or taking on a defensive winner's stance. In exasperation Sherry and her son, Todd, settled for a secondary choice of college because they got so bogged down in looking at every pro and con about each school. They failed to come up with a satisfactory compromise, and both ended up being disappointed in the final choice.

Withdrawer: You want to leave the scene in an argument. The first thing that comes to your mind when you feel a family conflict coming on is to remember you have something else you must do at that exact moment. The very fact that there is a fight in the home leaves you feeling anxious at such a level that you want to make a quick getaway. Once you leave the scene, you find your own way of dealing with the anxiety because you need space and time to think about what happened and to get rid of the bad feelings. When you come back home, you are sure the fight is over and everyone will go on as if the conflict never existed. One father Judy knows would leave for two hours, work out his feelings, come back home, open up the door and throw his hat in the kitchen to make sure the fight was over and the coast was clear. This had worked for his father, and he was sure it was the best way to deal with problems. Much to his surprise, he met even more hostility from his family when he entered the door. It was not acceptable for him to escape, since they wanted him to remain involved with them in dealing with the conflict.

Withdrawers believe that the best way to keep peace is to escape, but they soon learn that others in the family feel cut off and disregarded in the process. While it seems to solve things for the withdrawer, it makes things worse for other family members. When a father or a mother withdraws, adult children never learn how to handle the anxiety they feel at unresolved issues in the home. They may learn to act in (through physical complaints) or act out (escaping through addictive behaviors). The key factor for withdrawers is to give them the time they need away from the conflict but ask them to take responsibility by returning after the tension has dissipated so the family can deal with the conflict in a safe and productive way.

Resolver: You have high regard for relationships and high belief that the conflict can be resolved in a way that satisfies everyone. Because you put a great deal of energy into your emotional relationships with your family members, fights cause you great distress. Dissatisfied with making a compromise, you are eager to have conflicts resolved to everyone's satisfaction so you can once again have a close, emotional connection between family members. The anxiety you feel about disagreements in the home leads you to pursue others at all costs until there is mutual resolve. It is important that you talk things out, and you are persistent in keeping at it until there is some peace in the home. It is difficult for you to sleep or go on with other things until a solution is gratifying to all. There always seem to be things that are not exactly right between family members, so you are often bringing up relational issues. Due to your intensity, other members may react to your strong pursuer tendencies. They may try to keep you at bay, because you are always pointing out what is wrong in the relationship. Others need a reprieve from your constant concerns.

A resolver can teach adult children a lot about keeping one's personal relationships in a healthy growing place. Adult children may, however, resent the pursuer as an unnecessary intrusion into their lives. Janice is a pursuer, while her husband, Tim, and their son, John, are withdrawers. The male family members avoid her approach by staying away from home and keeping emotional boundaries. This only causes her to try harder, pushing them further and further away.

Obviously it is not only the conflicts but the style of doing battle that causes problems in the parent-adult child relationship. It behooves parents to recognize the unique style of each child and respond accordingly. A winner parent will get nowhere with a withdrawer child unless he or she can learn to be quiet, listen carefully and refrain from trying to persuade the child to accept the winner's point of view. Two withdrawers in a home must promise to come together after time away so they can deal with the problems together. The pursuer must learn to let the distancer distance, and the distancer must learn to come back at a later time. The compromiser, frustrated with a yielder who refuses to give an opinion, could ask the yielder to write down a list of what he or she desires and then make efforts to respond in those ways. Two winners may decide to let one talk on Tuesday and another talk on Thursday while the other one takes the role of listener. These are just a few ideas to break through conflict patterns that prevent parents and children from working toward good solutions concerning their differences. Each one will need to find unique ways to relate to one another in resolving the conflicts between them.

Finding Creative Solutions

Once family problems are recognized, the family has a great opportunity to deal effectively with them. The goal is to find a solution that can dissipate the negative energy that has piled up through past, hurtful interaction patterns. The family must do something different to break the old, hurting patterns and add something new in order to put creative solutions to work. Here are some ideas about how to get solutions started.

First, declare the problem and commit to the solution. Admit dissatisfaction about past ways of doing battle and indicate a desire to try new ways of relating. The following statements offer hopeful possibilities of change: "I withhold my affection when you don't do what I say, and I scold and shame you when you do something I don't like, but I'd like to change by accepting your thoughts and feelings so I can understand you better." "I've been trying to force you into my way of doing things, but I know your way is equally good, and I will affirm you rather than criticize you." "I realize I keep my distance by blaming you, and I will accept responsibility for my actions from now on. It's important to me to find good ways to connect." The confession initiates the change process. The vulnerable, about-face attitude opens others up in a way that can make a difference.

Then pay attention to the distinctive conflict style of each family member. We do not all behave in the same way when we are faced with disagreements. Some people seem to gain energy from a good argument, while others yield at the first sign of conflict. Some insist a compromise is always possible, while others flee without discussing the problem. Some believe that issues must be resolved so that everyone is happy; others want to win. Knowing what goes on internally for family members when conflict enters the relationship can be helpful in bringing opposing sides together to work on a problem.

Last, recognize family strengths and particular activities and behaviors that contribute to positive interaction. Discovering what the family is doing right is an important clue as to how to be creative in solving problems. By fostering the positive behaviors, the family will be able to work more effectively on the negative. The motto becomes "Keep doing those things that heal and quit doing the things that hurt."

Choosing to empower rather than to control or deciding to accept rather than shame automatically reverses the negative trends. Eliminating unrealistic expectations means a person is free to discover what he or she can do well and to learn what is appropriate for his or her particular age and situation. Being vulnerable in relationships invites others to come toward us rather than to keep their distance. Honest expression keeps us from hiding behind our masks.

An approach that focuses on solutions is hopeful. However, sometimes a family cannot get to future solutions until they have paid sufficient attention to the past hurts. In this case repentance is a necessary part of the solution process. Painful past events can continue to have a powerful negative influence unless family members admit the wrongs and begin to reestablish trust. After reconciliation, family members can put forth the remedial effort to make the desired changes. We will talk more about this in chapter eight.

A problem solved is a point of growth and celebration for the family. The solutions lead to a deeper level of intimacy in the family, which brings about more capacity for unconditional loving, acceptance and empowerment. Round and round it goes, one positive change contributing to another in an ongoing cycle of family unity.

Exercise
Identify your particular battle style and your adult child's style when you have differences. What does it take to be effective, and how will you make that happen?

8

When Disobedience Is the Chosen Path

....

There are times when no matter how carefully we talk with our young adults, they continue to choose a path that takes them away from Christ. There are areas in which God is quite clear about his will, and when our child chooses a path away from God it is painful to watch. The pain may be so great that we want to not have to observe it; cutting the child from our lives seems a choice of survival.

When our adult children turn from Christ, we need to treat them as we would any non-Christian we are in contact with. We show them the love of Christ and make certain we are available to point them in Christ's direction.

A friend told me (Boni) of her anguish over her daughter's promiscuity. It seemed every time they had contact Ellie learned of a different lover her daughter was involved with. Her friends at church insisted she should cut her daughter off and never see her again. They told her that to have contact with Sandy was condoning the sinful life

Sandy led. Ellie struggled with that approach. Was it wrong to show her daughter love? Sandy and Ellie had talked endlessly about Sandy's behavior and Sandy's relationship with Christ. Sandy knew where Ellie stood on the matter. Yet Sandy was an adult. Ellie had no control over her behavior.

Ellie chose to be in contact with Sandy. She believed that her task was to love her daughter as she would an unbelieving friend. Her hope was to win her back and to keep the path open for Sandy's return to faith. Ellie's expressions of love and caring were part of that hope, along with her continual prayers for her daughter's salvation.

The Effect on Parents

The choices our children make greatly affect us as parents. They may hope to be autonomous, and we may attempt to separate their decisions from our lives, but regardless we are affected. The potential for their happiness or sadness in a choice they make affects all parents who remain in loving contact with their children. This does not change when a child becomes an adult.

What do we do when we have done all we can to respectfully challenge a potential marriage, adventure or business deal and our child proceeds without our blessing? Just as we are beginning to adjust to the arrangement we notice the pain and anguish in their eyes and know they are in trouble. What is our role? Do we help, pretend we do not notice or stay out of it? Look at the following three typical scenarios many parents find themselves in with their adult children.

Marital Difficulties

It was the wedding of a lifetime. Seven bridesmaids and seven groomsmen surrounded the couple at the elegant formal ceremony. Seven hundred people attended. Everything was in its right place in the exquisite setting. The parents had gone all out for their daughter. Jim Glass, the father of the bride, had been a bit intimidated when his wife, Shirley, kept reminding him of the acceptable way to do things, but in the end he was glad they could provide for their only daughter. The Glasses had dreamed along with their daughter, Christine, about this affair. None of them had dreamed how big it would be or how much it would cost. But it all seemed worthwhile when they saw the smile on their daughter's face as she waved goodby from the limousine.

The marriage looked good five years later. The parents seemed satisfied that their daughter had married a man who would provide well for her and their new family. There were the usual differences and some stress over buying their new home. But the Glasses were able to provide the down payment, which alleviated the financial stress.

Everything had seemed so right. Can you imagine how shocked the Glasses were six months later when Christine pounded on their door in the middle of the night to ask if she and the children could stay the night? She broke down as she started telling the story. David had been gambling their money away, had lost his job and was becoming abusive. When he came home that night he had been beside himself with frustration, and she was afraid he would harm the children and her.

The Glasses needed time to take it all in. What was their responsibility at this point? Did they have a right to intervene?

This is not an uncommon story. Every day parents and grandparents are challenged with scenes similar to this. The Glasses had done everything they knew to ensure their daughter's happiness. Now everything was falling apart and what had seemed so right was going so wrong.

Parents are asking important questions about the place of empowerment in such situations. Was it enabling when the Glasses provided a down payment? Should they now open their home to their daughter and grandchildren, and for how long? How will they interact with their son-in-law and his family in this difficult situation? Is it possible they will be triangled in a negative way?

We Decided to Live Together!

Living together is one of the choices of adult children that parents find most difficult. As many of us interpret Scripture, sex before marriage is not an option for Christians. Yet many Christian parents find themselves called upon to respond to this choice.

Usually there are telltale signs that parents try to ignore or deny. If we do not approve of such a decision, our children try to keep secret for as long as possible their decision to live together. However, there comes a time when our eyes open wide enough to ask a direct question or our kids tire of the game and come out with the truth.

"Mom and Dad, I've met this neat guy. I'd like you to meet him. Can I bring him home this weekend?" Surely we are glad to meet the person our adult child wants us to meet. We may go out of our way to make arrangements for separate sleeping accommodations, only to find out they sneaked into one room during the night. It seems unnatural to be sleeping separately since they have been sleeping together for some time.

Janice was shocked when her son, Carter, asked if he and his girlfriend could meet her at the beach for a few days' vacation. A single parent, Janice said she would be happy to share her bedroom with Sara, but Carter immediately made it clear they would be camping together at the beach site. When Janice met them there, she felt rather awkward. She tried to have casual conversations with them but found herself tongue-tied the entire weekend.

John was flabbergasted because whenever he tried to call his son, his son's girlfriend always answered the phone. Finally he was brave enough to ask his son what the deal was. He found out they had been living together for more than three months, and his son intended to keep it that way. His girlfriend's parents had gotten a divorce when she was twelve years old, and she did not want to commit herself to a marriage, he explained to his father. That did not help matters for John. He could not understand that kind of reasoning and was angry that his son had settled for this arrangement.

Such stories come up often when you talk to middle-aged couples about their adult children, especially those in their late twenties and thirties. Each family will handle it differently, and there are many right ways to be helpful.

Susan, a widow for eight years, has another way of thinking about it. Her son, Greg, has been living with Vicki, a single parent with two grade-school-aged children, for the past year. It is his first serious relationship, and although Greg knows Susan is troubled with this choice, she understands his motive. Although she holds to the biblical standard of marriage before sex, she has listened to Greg explain his reasons for his behavior. He knows it takes time to ease into a ready-made family. He believes this living arrangement is stabilizing him as he takes gradual responsibility in the home.

Susan sees how Vicki's young children are beginning to trust Greg's kindness and friendship and are slowly allowing him into their lives. She knows that Vicki is not ready to say yes to marriage after her first failed relationship. Although Susan believes that Greg and Vicki would work through these issues more effectively and faithfully without cohabitation, she realizes that she has not and probably will not be able to change their minds. And she is concerned that she not destroy her relationship with her son (and Vicki), thus not only losing loved ones but also eliminating any possibility that she may be a godly influence in their lives.

Though Susan remains clear about her convictions, she also remains in relationship with Greg and Vicki. She commends and encourages their clear desire to achieve a permanent commitment and live together for life. She talks openly with them about what the marriage covenant can mean for them, though she listens carefully and respectfully to their ideas about where and when this will happen. She is very much a part of their family life, spending time with them during holiday celebrations and helping celebrate birthdays and other special events.

Sometimes it is difficult for Susan to talk to some of her friends at church who believe she is enabling her son's objectionable behavior. But she remains confident that it is important not to destroy the relationship and that she can still help her son and Vicki move toward an enduring marriage covenant.

A Business Deal!

The Andersons adopted their son, Chris, when he was eight years old. They were warned by their friends that it would be difficult to rear a child who had been abandoned and neglected. Familiar with the child development theory that emphasizes the importance of early bonding and attachment, they knew they had some major deficits to overcome. However, after having two children of their own, they were willing to take the risk, believing they had something important to offer this particular child.

They admitted, without hesitation, that Chris's growing-up years constituted an exceedingly stretching time for everyone. However, what the family learned about tolerance, patience, love and acceptance made a significant difference in their lives.

Dick and Betty were consistent in their love and support, even when it was hard to love and support Chris. Chris also persevered with his new parents. Having parents was not as easy as he had thought it would be. His parents saw his determination to make it through some rough situations. One of the proudest moments of their life was to see him walk across the stage to receive his bachelor of arts degree.

This was not the end of the Andersons' parenting, however. Although Chris had a college degree in business, the only job he could find was at minimum wage in a clothing store. Jobs were scarce. There was a prospect of working his way up into management, but the low salary was a constant reminder that it would be a long time before he could make the kind of money he thought would be possible with a college degree. Chris got an apartment with a couple of college roommates. The Andersons were understanding but encouraged him to learn what he could about business so he could make it on his own someday.

That day came sooner than anyone thought. A year later Chris took his parents out for dinner to tell them he had a friend who would help him finance his own business. He had all the plans laid out; he and his roommate would form a corporation and set up a small business in a nearby town. After conducting careful market research, they had found a place to rent, and everything was supposedly in order.

Without trying to break his bubble and his self-esteem, the Andersons asked questions, pointed out cautions and tried to help Chris think out his plans. They advised him to seek a lawyer's advice, since they were not familiar with all the ins and outs of starting a business. They worried that his decision was premature, but it was an opportunity and he was determined. They did what they could to show their support and love, as they had done all through his childhood.

Six months later Chris asked his parents out to dinner again. This time he was nervous and fidgety. He was ashamed and embarrassed to let them know that the person lending him the money had reneged. His parents' questions received discouraging answers. Chris did not have enough money to make his business rent payments, and he wondered if he could borrow from them.

Disappointed that Chris had waited so long to tell them about his business troubles and angry that he had been untruthful about some of what was happening, the Andersons needed time to think about how they could empower him in this situation. If they bailed him out, would this take away his initiative in trying to work out differences with his sponsor? Would there be a realistic end to the monthly need for their loan? Would facing the consequences of a bankruptcy be the best lesson for Chris? Would becoming partners in the business put Chris in a dependency pattern with them? These and many more questions went through their minds.

There were risks no matter what the Andersons decided to do. It was important that they take time to carefully think through all the ramifications. They needed to consider their own financial situation and be fair to their other children. They needed more facts and figures from Chris, so they would be clear about his situation. They would contact their lawyer to get an outside opinion and discuss this in their couples' group to get input about the emotional dependency issues.

There are no easy answers, and each situation between parents and adult children must be carefully evaluated with all facets of the decision clearly weighed.

Perhaps the most important thing the Andersons did when their son approached them was to listen. They let him know they were sorry for what was happening without casting shame or guilt his way. At the same time they were ready to be honest with their feelings and limitations. His integrity was at stake. They showed respect by letting him know they were proud of his accomplishments; they told him they believed he had what it takes to make a good businessman and they knew he could face these particular circumstances whether they were able to help financially or not. Likewise, he let them know that he knew it would be a gift of mercy should they be able to help in any way but said that if they were unable to help, he would understand and would not feel resentful.

Four Healing Principles

All families have problems. As we have seen, living together through the thick and thin of everyday life, family members will encounter struggles and stressors all along the way. Four common relationship problems that lead to ongoing problems in a family are conditional love, shame, control and distance. If a family is to function effectively, family members must first recognize and then learn to change these disruptive patterns.

Four healing principles that bring harmony between family members are covenant love (expressing commitment and faithfulness), grace (showing acceptance and forgiveness), empowerment (encouraging competence and growth) and intimacy (demonstrating closeness and communication; see Balswick and Balswick 1989). Knowing the difference between harmful and healing relationship dynamics will point families in the direction of health. Embracing these healing principles, family members will be able to combat the relational problems that cripple their functioning. Healing relationship principles will move family members toward well-being, whereas repeating the hurting patterns will move them toward further strife.

Unconditional love. Parents and grandparents who love their children and grandchildren unconditionally will support and help them in dire situations like the ones we have described. When adult children get themselves in difficult situations, it is not a time to close the door and shut them out. However, it is a time for parents to think critically and constructively as well as compassionately about what is the best way to be supportive. This takes a great deal of wisdom and often the help of trusted friends who can lend an objective perspective.

The eventual goal is to help adult children get back on track so they can make it on their own. We must take into account our own situation and the limits of what we can provide both physically and emotionally, but we will not turn away. There is no set prescription for what needs to happen next. Each situation may be a little bit different. But to offer compassion, unconditional love and emotional support is the first step.

Grace. To forgive and be forgiven is the hallmark of the Christian family. Unfortunately families often live under the cloud of shame rather than grace. In shaming homes family members set up a standard of perfection that is impossible to achieve. But when a family operates with acceptance and forgiveness readily available, grace reaches out to restore our members. For God so loved and cherished each unique created being that he gave his only Son for them. The intent was to restore and reconcile. Likewise, a family of grace will embrace each member as a unique, cherished creation of God. While they acknowledge human failure, they also take hope in the capacity for one to learn from mistakes and recover from imperfections. Repentance and forgiveness become redeeming ways to reconciliation, hope and life. Only when family members are loved, accepted and forgiven do they have the courage to begin anew.

Empowerment. We can take a great deal of hope in the fact that Jesus radically redefined the notion of power. The model in the New Testament is one of empowerment, or using power for others. Just as the Holy Spirit empowers Christians to live out the life of faith, family members are called to nurture, equip, instruct, confront, encourage and assist each other in the personal growth process. We feel this is such an important part of healthy family life that we have already dedicated an entire chapter to discussing it. When families are in conflict, it is important to keep empowering principles foremost in our minds. True resolution will be much more possible.

Intimacy. In a world that offers instant everything, it is difficult to take the time required to develop close relationships. It is easier to hide behind masks rather than to reveal oneself in open, honest ways. If the family is a place in which members experience rejection, the best way for family members to protect themselves from that kind of pain is to pretend they are okay when they are not. If members are loved only when they do acceptable things or shamed when they make mistakes or harshly punished when they fail, they will look for ways to anesthetize themselves from these condemnations. When denial and coverup become a way of life, family members are kept emotionally distanced from each other, and a barrier to intimacy limits the healing force in family relationships. When one is validated for being truly known, there is no need to cover up the truth, even when it is negative. Conflicts have a capacity to allow for constructive growth when family members are able to hear and respond with appropriate understanding.

It will always be a delicate balance to decide when you are helping and when you are hindering your adult children in crisis. There is no easy formula. But keeping doors open, communicating honestly and working together through mutual accountability and empowerment can bring about a deeper level of intimacy with our adult children.

A Debt That Cannot Be Paid

In *Da,* a profound film (1988) about an Irish father and his son, the son leaves home, finds a job and works hard so he can send money to his father. It is his way to pay back what he feels he owes to his parents. Without the son's knowledge, the father never spends a penny of the money he sends. Instead, at the father's death the son gets all the money back. The son is furious when he finds out, because now he will never be able to repay the debt he believes he owes. Distraught, he shouts at his father's grave: "I'll never forgive you for this, never! When did I ever get a chance to pay it back, to be out from under, to be quit of you?"

In *Families at the Crossroads* Rodney Clapp responds to this scene: But honest maturity requires admitting and embracing our dependence, accepting a debt that can never be canceled. No money can repay what our parents have given us. We would not be who we are or where we are without our family. Our best and truest hope is *not* to advance to some place where we owe nothing to our family, to create ourselves apart from all that has been given. Instead, our best and truest hope is to be freed to claim and accept what was given, to build on the good and redeem what is redeemable of the bad. What the gospel enables and expects is, in Karl Barth's words, not the destruction but the "radical renewal of the child-parent relationship," not the "separation of these kinsfolk" but their "genuine reconciliation, not merely in the peace of this transient world, but in the prospect of the perfection of the kingdom." (Clapp 1993:88)

A radical renewal is possible between parents and adult children when we have an eternal perspective. What we do as parents for our children in covenant love and empowerment is never something we expect to be repaid for doing. It is our call as kingdom people. Our hope is that our children will have the capacity to pass on this way of being in the world for the good of their children and humankind during their earthly lives.

Relationship at the Brink

Is there a time when parents are at the brink of a relationship? Do we come to a place where we have helped too much or have been asked to stretch too far? The Broadway musical *Fiddler on the Roof* helps us ponder these questions. How much change are we parents capable of tolerating? How much value difference can we accept? When are we at our limits of our hopes and expectations?

Tevye represents every parent who is asked to stretch to the limit in the midst of a world of tremendous change. He seems to be able to manage the political changes better than he can the personal. When it comes to his daughters there is too much at stake, too much to give up. He is able to give in, after much protest, when Tzeitel wants to marry a tailor instead of a rich man. He is obviously upset when Hodel, his second daughter, announces she is going to marry a radical who wants to overthrow the czar, but reluctantly he gives his blessing and permission.

But when Tevye's favorite and youngest daughter, Chava, marries a non-Jew, he can give no more. When Chava asks him to accept them he prays to God, "Accept them? How can I accept them? Can I deny everything I believe in? On the other hand, can I deny my own child? On the other hand, how can I turn my back on my faith, my people? If

I try to bend that far, I will break. On the other hand . . . there is no other hand. No, Chava. No-no-no" (Stein 1964:94-95).

This is the brink for Tevye. This is too much to ask, for his very value system is being challenged. He cannot flex at this point.

Most of us are asked to accept values and decisions of our children that make us angry and bewildered. But when it is in direct contrast to our basic value system, the Word of God, we are tested the most. There are some things we will never emotionally accept. This we must communicate to our children. But we still accept our children even when their choices lead them to consequences that are negative.

Value differences are an intolerable threat initially. But even when we disagree with the choice, we gradually accept the reality of that choice. When these choices take us to the breaking point, our relationship may be at the brink of disaster. We cannot give our blessing. There are times when it will be right and honest to not do so in these circumstances. Direct disobedience to God is not something to which we can give our blessing.

However, with covenant love we do not sever the relationship even when we cannot give a blessing. There is always hope that circumstances will change. It is no surprise that with a tear in our eye or lumps in our throat, we identify with Tevye, who disowns Chava but under his breath tells his oldest daughter to tell Chava, "God be with you!"

For Tevye, as well as for the father of the prodigal son Jesus describes in Luke 15, covenant love is the love that will bridge the estrangement that comes between parents and their offspring around choices that have serious and painful consequences. May God give us the grace to live in covenant love with our children and the courage to hold on to them through the difficult times in our relationship.

Exercise
Review the four healing principles discussed in this chapter. Choose one area to focus on improving through prayer and intentionally changing your behavior.

9

Boomerang
Children

•••••••••••••••••••••••••••

They're here, then they're gone, then they're back home again. It all seems to happen in a blink of an eye. Just when you have adjusted to the empty nest, it fills up again. A new phenomenon in our culture is adult children who return home after they've left home. How do we respond to this as parents? How can we help the returning home process be a growing experience rather than a regressive one? How do we cope with all those adults living together?

For some adult children, returning home after college or during other times of transition allows time to focus, make decisions and become better able financially to make it on their own. Others do not have the emotional maturity or resources to live on their own. They are not ready to take the step of independence that living apart demands.

Remembering that we are all different will help. There is no exact time when each child must be gone. In the United States this time is usually after schooling is completed. But in other countries the normal time might be sooner or later. In Northern Ireland, for example, it is rare that adult children would leave their parents' home before they marry. Culture has played a significant part in how independent a young adult needs to be and when. It may also be true that economics and other circumstances dictate that leaving-home date. In general families will treat each member as an individual with individual needs when it comes to working out the right time to leave.

Some adult children return home after having made the break, tried it on their own and failed in some way. They are in need of our help and often the protection our home can offer. Failed marriages, financial distress, addictions or medical problems are some of the common reasons these children cry out for parental help. Being a parent that can hear these cries and respond in some unique way is a goal most Christian parents have.

Shared Household

"Mom, Dad, I don't know how we're going to make it! I didn't want to tell you that Chuck had his driver's license revoked last month while driving under the influence. Now he's lost his job. I'm having to drive him everywhere, and it's driving us all crazy. Packing up the kids every time I need to take him somewhere is a terrible ordeal for all of us. Shelly hates to hear us say we're going anywhere in the car, and Eric screams his head off each time I put him in his car seat. I don't know what to do. We're at our wits' end. I don't think we're going to make it here in Utah. I don't know if our marriage will survive this."

One of the most painful experiences parents can have is to hear the distresses of their adult children. We want to believe they are well on their way to establishing a good living and managing their family. The last thing we want to hear is that they are in trouble. It seemed like it was just yesterday that we rejoiced with them in their new job, stood by their side on their wedding day or heard the great news that a new life came into their home. We were so proud to see them start out life on the right foot. How can everything seem so wrong? It's as if they're falling short before they've had a good chance to begin.

While there sometimes are obvious hints, parents typically keep their blinders on when adult children are having serious problems with addictions, financial struggles or their marriages. It's hard to face that their child is not making it on their own. This disappointment with life may be as hard for the parents to accept as it is for the child.

The truth hurts. We believe our adult children will no longer need to depend on us after they leave home. Then when they fail our pride is wounded. We speak in whispers to our friends and family about these problems. We feel embarrassed and ask ourselves the recriminating question *Where did we go wrong?* If they fail, we believe we fail.

Perhaps the first place to start when our adult children come to us for help is to honestly deal with our own feelings of failure about the situation. A place where we can admit the truth and share our anguish with others helps us begin to assess the situation for what it is.

It was in his couples' support group that Jim began his teary confession. "I don't know how to begin. Carolyn and I are devastated. We've just learned that our daughter is six months pregnant, and the father of her unborn child is seriously involved with another woman. They have no intention of getting married, they don't love each other, and Cinda will have the baby during her last semester of college. She has asked if she and the baby could live with us until she gets herself on her feet. We can't believe how stupid we've been about this. Why didn't we see the signs? Couldn't we have done something to prevent this? I feel guilty about being such a lousy father. I'm so angry about what's happening. I'm having a terrible time getting a grip on myself. Please pray for us." The group members were immediately sympathetic. Slow to speak but quick to offer compassion, they helped their middle-aged couple friends unfold the details and unleash their emotions. A few parents shared similar struggles they had with their own adult children. No one was there to throw a stone, for each parent could understand how life circumstances can lead to such predicaments.

The group offered prayers of support that night. But beyond this they offered practical help. There were notes of encouragement, phone calls, interactions during the next weeks and months that led to healing conversations. One person befriended Cinda so she had someone to confide in and walk with her through the difficult months that followed. The counselors at the Christian college were kind and helpful to all involved in this sensitive situation.

A few months later the parents' care group gave a surprise shower for the new grandparents, and a baby shower was given for Cinda by a special friend of the family. The group became an ongoing, safe place for Jim and Carolyn to work out the many adjustments that came with bringing Cinda and the new baby into their home. It also was a place to celebrate the wonderful rewards that came from bonding with their young grandson and for Jim to play a special role in his grandson's life. The three of them have worked out a living situation that is mutually satisfying. Cinda and her baby have been welcomed by the church, which has helped provide a child-care person when Cinda works. It's been an example of how a Christian community can be a resource to struggling families.

Love Tested

We may never have imagined how the concept of covenant love could take us to this particular edge. Does unconditional love require that we open our hearts and our homes to boomerang children, you might ask? The story of the prodigal son provides a model for us. In the face of having a disgruntled son leave home in an angry spirit, the father is able to get beyond the pain of rejection and open up his arms when he returns in his neediness. Imagine the shame the father must have experienced as he escorted his rebellious son through the small village back to his home. Everyone in the village had probably heard the screaming arguments and the disrespectful attitude of the son before he left. Everyone knew the father had every right to disown him and never take him back. But the father loved his son and based his actions on that love.

Parents' love will be tested not just in terms of whether we have the capacity to forgive and accept but whether we're willing to go the second mile and bring adult children back into our home. Do we throw them a feast or do we grudgingly accept them back in silent condemnation and subtle judgment? It is not easy to say yes, and it is often extremely difficult to say yes without an attitude. In a culture that places such a premium on independence, parents may feel they are doing a terrible thing when they take in their wayward, adult children. When we can get beyond using guilt to shape them up and when we get beyond castigating ourselves about what didn't we do right, then we have the potential of a creative exchange that can lead to healing.

Hostility or Hospitality

Recently I counseled a couple who remarried and brought children from a former marriage into the household. The stepfather was adamant that adult children should be on their own. This caused great distress for his wife, who placed a priority on her relationship with her children and concern about their welfare. When her daughter asked to come back home after traveling abroad for a year, it was an automatic yes in her mind. She never anticipated that her husband would take such a strong and (in her mind) rigid view of this situation. As you can imagine, it caused a great deal of disruption in their relationship. Under these circumstances, the returning adult child definitely started out on the wrong footing. Resentment filled the household when she and her stepfather were in the same room, causing frustration and anguish for all concerned. Had the couple been able to talk openly about this prior to their marriage, it could have spared them some painful arguments.

So is it hospitality that we offer our children when they come back home? Do we have an attitude toward them that is hospitable or hostile? Most often boomerang children have been hurt in a world that's filled with hostility and hard circumstances. Perhaps they've become hardened, distrustful and suspicious when they've tried to make a go of it and fallen flat. With hospitality as an attitude of our hearts, we can reassure and restore them in their time of turmoil. If our homes become a place of shelter that brings hope to our weary adult children we have achieved something extra special.

Parents must work toward creating a free and friendly space where these adult children can enter our homes and be befriended by us. The attitude of hospitality invites them to come home on their own terms rather than imposes our terms on them. This means we must work together to build a household of mutual understanding and respect. It's not that we become neutral but that we provide a welcoming space where we are flexible enough to work toward balance and harmony.

Making a Tough Choice

For obvious reasons the decision to have our adult children boomerang home is not something we take lightly. We need time to think out a plan that has potential for success. Also, there is no one right way for any particular family, which means the unique circumstances of each situation must be carefully weighed. We believe wisdom often comes through a collaborative effort among parents, adult children and objective sources from outside the family. Boomeranging home may not be the best option for some adult children, and saying no does not imply a conditional love. A covenant commitment may require that parents stand firm with a particular child, since they believe it is not in that adult child's best interest to come back home. For others grace is extended, and it is exactly what the adult child needs to have a new start in life.

Many parents in midlife are in the throes of making decisions about taking in their boomerang kids. Our adult children's unfortunate situations require that we consider how taking them back can be an empowering rather than enabling experience. We want communal living to be an enriching solution when they come back to live with us. It's not simply a matter of having their old room back; it demands that they come back as an adult into a changed household. Let me (Judy) share what we learned from our experience of taking our daughter, Jacque, and her family back into our home ten years ago.

When our daughter and her family spent three years living in our home, we decided to conceptualize the arrangement as shared household living. Although we owned the home, her family rented a specific space in the home that included bedrooms, bathroom and living area. We shared several common rooms in the home: formal dining and living room, kitchen, laundry, bathroom and study. My husband and I had a separate bedroom, bathroom and living area in the upstairs of the house. Obviously, it helped to have a large house.

We determined such things as who would cook meals on what days, who would clean up after meals, standards about how to maintain the household and yard, who did what chores, and so on. Each aspect of our shared living would be a cooperative effort. Weekly household meetings helped us work out details and the inevitable kinks that came up with our new living arrangements. We included the children in these meetings, since they were a vital part of the extended household. We made efforts to take their needs into account as well as to pay attention to how they would make positive contributions to the atmosphere of our home. Even though they were quite young at the time (two and three years old), it was essential that they were included as an integral part of the arrangement.

Lessons in Boundaries

I believe working out boundaries with boomerang children is one of the most crucial areas that will make or break household living. We have explained this concept in chapter three, but sharing living space with other adults requires additional understanding. These delicate places that define personal territory must be regarded with great respect.

In our shared home, clearly defined areas gave Jacque's children permission to play freely and also gave grandparents assurance of comfortable adult space. My husband and I were grateful for our private living room, which defined our special couple relationship. Since we both had full-time jobs outside the home, we needed a reprieve from the high energy of a family with young children. A place where we could relax and enjoy quiet time either alone or as a couple was fundamental to our emotional health. Our daughter's family needed a sense of privacy around their family unit as well. We respected each other's need for separation as well as provided places of togetherness in the common areas.

Boundaries taught all of us the importance of honoring each person's private territory. The rule of the home was to knock before entering anyone's private room. Of course, the children went by the letter of the law! When the doors to our living area were open, they took great joy in their freedom to enter in and jump in our laps. But when the doors were closed, they were sure to knock first.

We also established a clearly defined boundary around our role as grandparents to our grandchildren. We wanted it to be clear to the children that their mother and father were the leaders of that family unit when it came to nurture and discipline. This gave us the privilege of doting and spoiling them like normal grandparents. When Jacque and Bill were absent, we took on parenting responsibility. Then when Jacque and/or Bill returned we were glad to return that role to them. One day Curtis made the astute observation, "When Mommy comes home she'll tell me what to do, but now you tell me." It didn't take their young minds long to understand who was in charge when, and they adapted very well. We were not the surrogate parents but the grandparents of our grandchildren. In the grandparenting role we gave them extra attention and nurture to complement what they were receiving from their parents. I'll have to admit that sometimes we had to bite our tongues when we disagreed with how their parents were handling certain situations, but we removed ourselves from the scene, physically and emotionally, so there would be no confusion about who were the leaders of their home.

Privacy in bedroom and bathroom space is another matter to be determined. Whether one decides on locked doors or a policy of knocking before entering, respect for others is the golden rule. One day not long after Jacque and family came to live with us, Curtis and Jacob came into my bathroom to watch me get ready for work. While I was putting on my makeup they were touching my bottles of perfume and other things. I found myself saying, "Don't touch that, that's Grammie's!" and "Don't touch that, it might break!" After a little while three-year-old Curtis turned to me and said, "And Grammie, you don't touch our stuff either!" Well, I giggled inside but used this as the perfect opportunity to help them understand how we would honor their personal boundaries. I happily let him know that I wouldn't touch his stuff without permission and that I would knock at the door of his bedroom or playroom before I barged in, just as I was asking him to do. We made a pact that morning that was a wonderful lesson to us throughout the years.

It goes without saying that a high regard for boundaries extends to such things as personal mail, phone calls, personal belongings, relationships with friends and financial matters. These are places that need protecting. We must not be intrusive because we live together under one roof. I remember the time I made a comment to my daughter about a piece of mail that looked like an overdue credit card bill. This violation of boundary was a breach between us until I could ask forgiveness and correct the error of my ways.

These principles help when boundaries have been violated:

☐ Address what, when and how a boundary was violated.

☐ The person who violated the boundary must acknowledge the violation.

☐ Decide what amends will restore trust.

☐ Respecify the boundary.

☐ Recommit yourselves to keeping established boundaries.

☐ Change your behavior to show commitment to the boundaries.

☐ Be accountable to the entire family.

Making Mutual Contracts

Agreeing ahead of time about expectations and responsibilities saves many headaches. The following discussion is an example of how these concrete areas can be negotiated.

Our *shared space* was open to all, and each had the right of equal access. We respected this space by keeping the area clean and uncluttered, since everyone would use it. Items in this area were for everyone's use, so we tended to keep it free from personal or private objects. We decided that anyone could request the area for a special party or event by setting dates and times in advance and clearing it with the household. That gave each family the opportunity to invite friends over and to be able to function as a nuclear family without the rest of us needing to be involved.

It's amazing what issues can be stirred up around *eating and food*. Perhaps it's a reminder of earlier days when the parents provided for these basic needs of their dependent children. They not only gave shelter, clothing and food but also determined everything about these matters. Buying food and clothes puts one in control of what children eat and wear. Whether it's a matter of nutritional values, tastes in the kind of clothes to wear or how to furnish a house, adult children will have their own ideas, which may be in distinct contrast to family values of the past. If these issues are ignored, watch for a major fight soon after the boomeranger arrives.

When food is bought and prepared as a common venture, it will take some careful negotiation. Cooking and eating food together is a wonderful way to nurture and show love, so it can lead to lovely connection and communion around the table. The daily and weekly menu and food purchasing will need to be decided. Should boomerang children decide they would rather eat alone or as a separate unit, they will buy and eat what they choose without parents commenting or criticizing these choices. Perhaps having occasional meals together is a nice compromise, for it offers times of connection as well as allows for separation. When the family eats meals together, it is important to determine ahead of time who is responsible for the planning of the meal, the buying of the food, the preparing of the meal and the clean up. Having a weekly or monthly meal together, in which members take turns preparing the dinner for the others, is a nice way of giving of oneself for others in the household.

It is most helpful to have personal shelves in the refrigerator and cupboard space for each family unit. There can be common use of spices, major items like salt, sugar and flour, and dishes, pots and pans. Freedom to borrow from each other can be clarified by leaving a note and letting the other know the item will be replaced.

Another area for negotiation is the handling of household *money*. Together the adults will decide if or how rent is to be paid, mutual paper products are bought and other financial areas will be covered. Be certain that the contract is clear in these areas. Putting it in writing for all to negotiate will help in keeping things clear.

Household Responsibilities
Taking responsibility for safety and protection of the household is also important. Sally opened up her apartment to her adult son a year after

college graduation. She was appalled that he was irresponsible about the safety of her home. As a single person, she had a routine of keeping the home secure with window and door locks. When Jonathan was lax about these rules, it was a personal injury to her. She couldn't seem to help him recognize how vulnerable she felt when she found the door unlocked at three a.m. Sally felt that being responsible for the safety of the home showed regard for each of them. This became clear when their apartment was robbed during a weekend Sally was visiting a friend. Jonathan not only was humbled by that event but also realized his error when he had to replace the CD player and video equipment that were taken from the home. From that day on there was never a question about taking seriously his responsibility in that area.

There is also need to be responsible when it comes to everyday routines like keeping washers and dryers empty and ready for the next person, emptying the dishes from a dishwasher or keeping the kitchen clean. These tasks indicate consideration for all members of the family. Keeping stereo and television noise to an agreeable level, taking care with getting-up or going-to-bed rituals, and sharing shower and bathroom space are areas to be negotiated and regarded with sensitivity.

Emotional Atmosphere

Daily interaction between family members determines the emotional climate in the home. A pleasant "good morning" and "good night" can make all the difference in the world when it comes to having a pleasant household atmosphere. Conflicts and negative emotions are to be expected in any family, but learning to deal effectively with the conflicts is the key to harmony in the home. When negative emotions are denied or ignored, it takes a toll on everyone. Grumpy faces and subtle martyr messages influence the emotional environment. When we fail to deal with our conflicts, we will have difficulty knowing how to come to any resolution (see chapter seven for principles of resolving conflict). The goal of the extended family is to work toward harmony.

Household Goals

The old adage "If you don't know where you're going, you'll never get there" is an important reason to establish household goals, whether it's to envision new ways to relate to one another in family relationships or to make plans about how to celebrate a holiday. Setting goals will help you achieve what you want to have happen in your household. A family without a sense of direction wavers to and fro, letting external circumstances determine the future. A proactive family will make long- and short-term goals to turn their dreams into reality.

We invest ourselves in that which we hold precious. A purposeful goal not only helps a family identify what's important for them but also helps the family implement ways of attaining their values. Good intentions are never enough. A family needs to agree on specific objectives that will help them accomplish what they care about in terms of household living. Families who work together toward common goals have a deeper meaning that enriches their family life. Whether it's making plans for a birthday celebration, solving a family problem or accomplishing a specific task, a family reaches a deep sense of satisfaction when they join together in this common effort. As each family member contributes to the family as a whole, he or she is appreciated for the unique part that person plays. The family that works together for common goals reaps the family rewards of closeness and unity.

Goal-Setting Helps

How does a household go about setting goals? Establishing a family council is a good place to start. This involves setting aside a place and time for household members to come together to share ideas about needs, values and desires. Using the brainstorming approach, each member is encouraged to freely contribute any and all ideas that come to mind. The invitation to think outside the lines brings up many creative possibilities. One person keeps a list of all ideas and even the most outrageous suggestions. Every person, from oldest to youngest, is taken seriously in this information-gathering process. This exercise brings each person into the process so that goals are cocreated.

Next, choose one goal from among the many ideas through a consensus. Narrowing down the field can be difficult, but it is necessary to prioritize. Once the main goal is established, the family can now begin to brainstorm about the specific behaviors that are needed to accomplish this goal. The family formulates subgoals (specific objectives) that will help them execute the greater goal. Subgoals need to be both realistic and doable. Brainstorming once again is the best way to elicit a number of imaginative ideas. Once all the ideas are listed, each suggestion must be evaluated in terms of whether it is reasonable and desirable for the whole family. In other words it's a question of whether the family will be successful in following through.

Celebrating birthdays was an enjoyable family goal. We brainstormed all the ideas about how we would make that happen. The kids were excited and had many thoughts about what would make celebrations good, all the way from balloons to party hats and whistles. I decided that cooking a favorite meal for the birthday person was a good idea. Jack and Bill were adamant about having a special birthday cake and ice cream, while Jacque thought a special birthday plate would add a nice touch. What a wonderful bunch of ideas we had, and that began one of the nice traditions of our new household. It was something we all looked forward to doing together, and we thoroughly enjoyed each celebration. One of the concessions Jacque and I wanted was to make sure all the nonbirthday adults did the cooking rather than rely on either her or me to do that work. We agreed to share the responsibility and involved the kids in setting the table and putting out the fancy napkins and party favors.

After they agree about the specifics, members must commit themselves to keeping their part of the bargain. When goals are coevolved, it's relatively easy for individuals to cooperate. Clear, written objectives help everyone know exactly what's expected of them as they agree to clinch the deal.

Making the Agreement and Sticking to It

Once the goal and subgoals are set forth in specific objectives and tasks are established, a contract can be signed to signify mutual commitment. This final step gives all family members a chance to promise that they will make every effort to do their part. This can be done by signing a written contract made up by the family or by shaking hands at the end of the family council. The essential thing is that each person agrees to the conditions set forth and promises to keep the contract.

It's also vital to specify a time frame for this contract. Whether it's one month or six months, it's best for the family to periodically review progress. Meeting each week for family council is a good way to evaluate the effectiveness of the contract. The family asks itself, "How are we doing? Are the objectives helping us meet the goal? Is there anything that needs to be changed?" These questions allow for needed correctives and innovative suggestions. An ongoing fresh perspective will continue to improve or reshape the subgoals.

When problems occur, the family must also agree to come back to the drawing board (family council) to renegotiate. This is not to be a time of blaming or defensiveness but a chance to make things better. The thing to figure out is why a breakdown occurs. Recognizing barriers (were the goals too high?), considering various courses of action (what can we change?) or looking to alternatives (what haven't we tried?) helps the family figure out a new course of action. Since goals can be reached in a number of ways, changing immediate small steps is often the best way to assure achievement of the long-range goals. Minor setbacks are to be expected. Therefore failure is viewed not as a catastrophe but as an opportunity to regroup and try again. Flexibility is the key. Listening is the best path to ingenious solutions. It may be that encouragement, instruction or equipping is needed. It is a time for family members to recommit themselves, to join hands and to take up the task once again.

Family goals are only as effective as the family's commitment to each other. Steps of action toward long- and short-range family goals requires that each member reach beyond individual desires. Family members must work together to be a family unit. Just as the apostle Paul explains, each unique part has something essential to offer the whole body of Christ, and no one part can function effectively without the others. When we give of ourselves, set apart time, put forth effort and contribute our special giftedness, we serve the whole. Converting our values into goals requires a vision. Family members must draw a landscape, plant the seeds, remove the obstacles and play their unique part in making their ultimate family dream a living reality.

A Way Station

What we can offer to our adult children when they need extra support is a way station. It is rewarding to be able to give them a new start in life, help them through a difficult transition or help them overcome a hurdle in life. In some cases, however, the opportunity we offer may not lead to increased responsibility. This is the risk we take. But we believe it is better to have tried and failed than to have not tried at all. When the arrangement is not effective, we may need help to put an end to the original plan. If an adult child is unwilling to give up a chemical dependency, for example, parents make matters worse by providing an easy situation that prolongs their irresponsible behavior. Then we become enablers rather than empowerers. There are times when parents still will choose to stand by the innocent victims in these situations, that is, young children or a spouse who is trying to break the dependency bond with the irresponsible person.

Every parent will need to evaluate the situation of taking in adult children according to their own resources and limitations. Sometimes, even though we do the best we can, it is not enough. Other times we can offer just enough to get our kids started in the direction of change. Then it has been a privilege to know we've made a difference in their lives by offering additional support. In addition we reap benefits like bonding with our grandchildren and establishing more positive relationships with our adult children.

It is challenging to stretch ourselves in new ways and open ourselves to new knowledge about our children and who they are becoming. Mutual understanding and respect become the foundation of the friendship to come. We have a chance to grow from the boomerang experience. My husband and I have benefited from being with our grandchildren at the most impressionable years of their lives. We have an affection and connection with them that we wouldn't trade for anything in the world. Our relationship with our daughter, which had been quite strained during her adolescence, is now one of quality and trust. Although it didn't save her marriage, it did offer her family a stable situation in which they could recoup from a highly stressful situation. In addition it gave Jacque an opportunity to finish her college degree and develop herself as director of a daycare center. Our grandsons are doing well in school, happy with their new home and community three hundred miles from us. It delights us that they love to visit and go on summer vacations with us. We have a history of shared living experiences that we cherish. I've written a journal about their young lives that I will give to them when they are older. I've kept scrapbooks and videotapes of these wonderful years as a shared household.

Home: A Place of Restoration

If our home is a place of restoration for our boomerang children, it will have potential to deepen their connection with us and with God as well. Giving them a second chance to reach their potential, to deepen and broaden their insights, can offer them a new lease on life. When we share both the wealth of our experiences and good fortune, they may find the courage needed to face their fears and develop a centeredness in Christ that helps them breathe with confidence once again.

Perhaps the most important way we create understanding is to be vulnerable in our interactions with our adult children. When we are in touch with how we too have been affected by fears of rejection, doubt and insecurity about our abilities, we open up possibilities of interpersonal sharing. When we help them look at their life experiences with eyes and ears of acceptance and hope, we offer them a chance to find their intuitions and strengths that can move them forward. And we learn more about ourselves as we give of ourselves and are receptive to what they give to us. Our children need to know that they bring something important to us when they return home. In this mutual interaction we will come to know ourselves and our children through and through, including joys and pains, pleasures and sorrows, ups and downs, highs and lows. This interactive process shapes our character.

When you think about it, it is quite a privilege to know our adult children this intimately, wounds, warts and all. Listening compassionately to them and resonating through similar experiences of woundedness gives hope that failures can be redeemed and spring forth new life. When we can hear their story of pain, they are able to reflect on that pain with less fear. And pointing out their hidden gifts and talents gives them permission to believe in themselves again. That's when they can take hold with renewed force and make new things happen.

Our most important contribution as parents is to offer a friendly space where our kids can relive their story. The hospitality we offer is the essential piece we have to give. When we ask them to enter as themselves, we give them a chance to discover themselves anew. In Henri Nouwen's words, we allow them to "sing their own songs, speak their own languages, dance their own dances; free also to leave and follow their own vocations" (Nouwen 1975:51). If our home is to be a redemptive place, it must be an open, receptive place where something can happen to us as well. We must let go of our need to be in the driver's seat and pay attention to their inner voices. We need to create a space and invite them to enter into a new relationship with us.

In an attitude of humility and hospitality, we offer them promise of discovery. Here the safe boundaries of love and acceptance can lead to self-discovery. Listening to their inner selves, they can draw from inner strengths and find their way once again. When they leave home a second time, they'll be better equipped. Boomerang children must be more than guests in our home. We must embrace them as God's children who are finding their way. It is more than an obligation; we become guides alongside them in their search for truth and understanding. Rather than give them the solutions, we point them to One who can help them find their way and come to grips with their lives.

Exercise

Take a moment to meditate on how your home is a place of restoration for your adult child(ren). How can you sharpen your eyes and ears of acceptance and love to help them find courage to restore their lives? Determine one or two specific things that will help them know you hold them precious in your mind and heart.

10

Newly Formed Families

····························

Eventually most of our children leave our home and in one form or another establish homes of their own. In those places they set the tone and the rules and have the authority. We become the visitors hoping for a hospitable welcome. In many instances we look with pride on this new family and thank God for bringing our child to maturity and independence. In other cases our child has not followed in God's way, and we grieve. In either situation our hope is that we will be faithful in our interactions with them and that our behavior will show love to this newly formed family.

Many of us have anticipated the day our adult children will fall in love (with someone we like) and marry as they establish themselves in adulthood. It was the ideal of our generation: two adults, preferably both Christian, marry, live on their own and eventually have children. This gave most of us meaning, and so we dream this same dream for our adult children. In spite of our hopes, however, many young adults are doing things quite differently. Some postpone marriage until they are in their forties, some choose not to have children, some remain single, some cohabit. How do we respond to this variety of choices of our children's generation?

The Newly Formed Couple

Wedding bells ring in the news that a new couple has joined in holy matrimony. Our dreams have come true, and we stand at our son's or daughter's side as they pledge themselves to each other, we hope for life. However, once the honeymoon is over, we soon realize we must make some major adjustments. Even though we know a lot about married life and have worked through relationships with our parents and parents-in-law, there will be some new challenges for us to face. For a start, how are we to relate to this new member of the family? Supposedly we have a new daughter or son, yet it does not feel that way. We feel a bit strange about relating to this relative stranger who has won our adult child's heart. And we are awkward around the family of our new daughter-in-law or son-in-law.

Carl Whitaker describes the wedding as a time when two families send out their best representative to win over that new spouse to their family ways. This statement makes us chuckle, but we also realize the truth that is tucked behind it. Usually two families of two different cultures come together that day, sometimes clashing. Even when they blend exceptionally well, each family represents different traditions and ways of being that will cause friction.

I (Judy) remember how difficult it was for my Swedish mother-in-law to accept my Italian sister-in-law because she was more verbal and outgoing than the more reserved Scandinavians. What makes a good in-law, and how do we go about learning these new roles? Exactly what will the new spouse call me? How will we take on the role of mother-in-law or father-in-law role without becoming the dreaded outlaw? How will we be expected to treat our married son or daughter to assure the new spouse we want to be supportive but not intrusive to their newly formed family?

What is more, what about becoming grandparents? Will our children expect us to baby-sit, and will we meet the test when it comes to disciplining them? Finally, although we feel quite competent in the childrearing department, childrearing practices have changed, and our ideas might be considered old-fashioned. Perhaps they will not want to hear our words of wisdom. Even this typical new family feels untypical to us. How will we meet this challenge with our adult children?

Welcome to Our Family

Is it possible to welcome a daughter-in-law or son-in-law into the family as one would welcome a child of our own? Is that the goal we hope to achieve? James T. Burchaell makes the following statement: "The only home which is safe for anyone to be born into is the home that is ready to welcome someone who does not belong there by right of kinship, but belongs there in virtue of hospitality" (quoted in Clapp 1993:149). If he is right, that covers a lot of territory. Welcoming the spouse of one of our children would certainly be part of the hospitality offered.

What does welcoming a new son-in-law or daughter-in-law involve? To say that we will treat this new member of the family as we treat our own child seems a bit naive. Many parents have annoying habits that their children tolerate because they love them and know their parents are much more than any particular annoyance. Our children have graciously learned to ignore the unlovely in us and the negative comments that inadvertently pop out of our mouths from time to time. We have a long-standing relationship with our children that has weathered offenses on both sides, and we have come to an understanding that only time could produce. Our child's new spouse does not share that history with us. The relationship then is much more fragile.

A woman in a support group was talking about her fear about her son's coming marriage. Mostly she was afraid of being a terrible mother-in-law. She was unclear about what that role involved and desperately desired to escape the awful stereotype that we hear about. Boni's friend Debby assured her that did not need to happen. Debby loves her mother-in-law dearly. She clearly believes she has the best mother-in-law in the world. The outstanding characteristic is Mom O'Neill's consistent positive feedback. If Debby paints the living room, Mom O'Neill thinks she has done a great job. If Debby tries a new menu, Mom O'Neill thinks it tastes great. If Debby is overwhelmed with parenting, Mom O'Neill lets her know she believes in her ability to do it well. If Debby wants advice, Mom O'Neill will give that too but only if she is asked. In her consistent affirming of Debby as a person, a mother and a partner for her son, Mom O'Neill has earned the right to speak the truth (positive or negative) to Debby in love.

I (Boni) am trying to make Mom O'Neill my model. I want to let the spouses of my children know I approve of them. I want them to know that their way of doing things is fine and it is not I who must be pleased in the relationship. I do not want to be an added burden to the first years of my children's marriages. But of course none of us do. And yet the in-law problem is a real one that I often hear discussed by clients in marital therapy.

It is difficult for our son to be pulled in two directions between the parents he loves and the spouse he has made the priority in his life. Yet parents' behavior often puts children in that situation, often unknowingly. We need to give the new couple enough space to develop their own flow of things without giving those subtle or unsubtle messages that they still owe us their loyalty. This can happen all too easily.

I remember hearing of a major conflict between a newlywed wife and her mother-in-law. This couple had invited the husband's parents over for dinner one evening, and Myra was quite nervous about it. At one point her mother-in-law made an offhand comment about the instant rice. And she was right, it was instant, the way Myra's family always made rice. Her mother-in-law went on, "Well, this is a first for me. Next time I'll teach you how to make real rice." Myra was not only embarrassed but also devastated by the comment. She heard it as criticism and was humiliated. Later, when her husband, Jeff, tried to defend his mother, it made Myra even angrier. She felt Jeff would always take his mother's side, and that did not feel good. The argument escalated, and Jeff felt the anguish of being pulled between the two women in his life who meant the most to him. It seemed the only way out was to agree with Myra and hate his mother. *She won't be happy with anything less,* he thought to himself. He was angry, feeling that Myra had trapped him into compromising himself for the sake of peace.

Any one of us is capable of making a statement like Jeff's mother's. Even if we said such a thing without malicious intent, it sets up a barrier of misunderstanding. How careful we need to be to hold our tongues and recognize the insecurity of any young couple to anything that smacks of criticism. The couple needs time to establish a boundary around their relationship that strengthens their bond of interdependence. Becoming a new entity where they can determine likes and dislikes of their own, learn unique patterns of relating and create traditions that tighten their union is an important part of solidifying that marital boundary. The biblical idea of leaving parents to cleave to a spouse clarifies this process. We cannot be too careful initially. We must earn the right to enter their newly formed family at their invitation. It never is accomplished from a position of authority. Our authority days are over.

In Times of Conflict
A few years ago Todd and Alison were married, to the delight of Alison's parents, Jim and Margie Washburn. Todd was the son Jim and Margie had never had. Alison is an only child, and Jim was thrilled to have another male in the family to do things with. Like his father-in-law, Todd is an amateur mechanic and loves being under the hood of a car. Together they rebuilt a few old cars for Todd to sell, helping the young couple earn a little extra money.

In the fifth year of the marriage there seemed to be an irreconcilable difference. Jim and Margie did not know what to do. They did not know what their role should be during this marital dispute. Alison was demanding their loyalty. After all, she is their daughter. Yet Todd had been so close to the family, especially to Jim. Were they to cut him off at this point? They were confused about what was right because they were pulled in both directions.

This is a problem many parents face in dealing with their adult children. If you made it through the leaving transition in a positive way, it is likely that you have been able to maintain a friendship relationship with your child that has continued through the newly formed marriage. Don't blow it now. Although you have been able to talk to your adult child as a friend when he or she confides in you, now you must honor their marital union. There will be complications unless you are willing to speak openly to them together. It can be tempting to triangle yourself, and even with the best intentions it takes away from the marital dyad working out their own problems.

I (Judy) remember getting caught in such a situation with my daughter. When my son-in-law talked with me about their marital problems, it did nothing but further muddy the waters between them. My daughter questioned not only my loyalty to her but also my loyalty to their marriage. Whenever a parent takes sides, it leaves one spouse at a disadvantage. My daughter felt she had been ganged up on, even though, in my mind, I was trying to make things better for her. I learned a good lesson that day. Once I had gotten involved in that way, they had to deal with not only their relationship but also my part in the triangle.

Never bend your ear to one spouse without the other's being present. If you do, it will lead to an even deeper mess. If they ask for your input, get them together, listen with an open mind, admit your biases and give your impressions as honestly as you can. Then leave the scene, respecting the fact that they must find a resolution between themselves. Do what you can to support them in that resolve.

I (Boni) met with Natalie and Roger in marital therapy for several months and watched them put back together a marriage that had gone bad. It had been a difficult time for them, but they were committed to making it work and getting beyond the problems they had in their marriage. But then we came to a standstill. Natalie could not get over the hurt of being cut off from Roger's family when he had moved out. His mother did not return her calls, said mean things to other members of the family about Natalie and clearly took Roger's side, even though she had no facts to go on. Roger wanted his parents back in their lives, and Natalie was having a hard time with that. How could she invite them to dinner after all they said about her? How could she pretend to be a daughter to them when they had so quickly taken sides against her? She felt the relationship between them was destroyed, and only her love for Roger allowed her to even consider involvement with them again. It took a lot of negotiation to finally get to a place of agreement.

Befriending the Relationship

Perhaps the best way parents of married children can relate to their children in marital conflicts is to befriend the marriage relationship through the conflict. In this way they do not take a stand for or against either partner but take a stand for what the two young adults have formed together, the marriage.

Jim and Margie attempted to do just that. They decided to try and maintain contact with both Todd and Alison. They believed that Todd and Alison could work things out, and they wanted to affirm their belief in that marriage. The Washburns wanted their behavior to stand for the marriage. They decided to not take a stand with Alison against Todd or with Todd against Alison but rather a stand for the marriage Todd and Alison had.

Once the Washburns began thinking of the marriage as a separate entity to be nurtured and preserved, that clarified the role they wanted to take with Todd and Alison. As their interactions and conversations continued through the months ahead, they often asked themselves, *Will my action be of help to the marriage?* The answers to this question gave them solid principles to follow.

And Then There Were Three

The next newly formed family is the family after children come into the home. This is a highly stressful time for most families. Especially in dual-earner homes, everyone seems to be on overload. I remember a good friend talking about how much she adored her husband right after they were married. She used to wake up in the morning, look at

Glen's beautiful body and think how fortunate she was to be married to him. After five years of marriage and three children, she now talks about how exhausted she is from giving so much to her young children each day. Now, when the shrill cry of their newborn wakes them in the morning, she turns to Glen and says, "Get that beautiful body out of bed and get our crying baby!"

Perhaps the most important thing we can now do as parents is to appreciate the great amount of stress young families are under. Understanding the amount of effort it takes for a young couple to manage the demands of work and family means a lot to them. It is a prime time when they need extra help and support, and we may be the ones who are able to give it. Such things as taking the children for an evening, having the family over for a meal, doing a few errands or driving children to their appointments can make a difference. We can lift their exhaustion level by helping them with household matters such as painting a room, fixing the plumbing or helping with spring cleaning. Offering to take grandchildren on short trips provides a needed break and gives the couple some alone time. If we care about strengthening their marriage, we will do all we can to ensure that they have time together. I know of parents who pay for a yearly marriage enrichment weekend for their children (as well as take care of the kids), which shows how much they care about their children's marital relationship.

Who Knows Best?
Whatever we do for our grandchildren must be done in accordance with their parents' approval. We can still get in trouble, even when we offer help, if we do it in the wrong way. One grandmother I know decided to cut her granddaughter's long hair into a pixie style without consulting the child's mother. This presumptuous act understandably caused a breach between them that lasted for years. If we presume grandchildren are ours to do with as we please, we are mistaken. They are not ours; they are our children's children, and the parents must decide what is best. We must ask, offer and invite, not assume, act or demand. We must learn to be sensitive to the needs of our newly formed family.

A friend was telling me how blessed she felt to have such a good relationship with her daughter-in-law, Jessica. They had become great friends in the three years of this young marriage. When Nina visited me a few years later, things had changed drastically. Her son and Jessica had a child. While Nina thought Jessica was a great mother, she did not seem to be able to communicate that to Jessica. It seemed Jessica took everything as criticism. If Nina held the baby when he fussed and asked if he was hungry, Jessica thought she was being critical. If Nina offered to baby-sit, Jessica thought her mother-in-law thought she could not take care of her own child. If Nina bought by a cute outfit for her grandson, she would never see him in it. Nina had loved being a mother-in-law, but being a grandmother was turning into a nightmare.

Not everyone has as much trouble as Nina had in trying to be a good grandparent. But being perceptive and sensible about how we interact around the grandchildren is crucial. Again, our role is a supportive one. If we attempt to be anything other, we are overstepping our role. Here are some guidelines to follow:

☐ Decisions regarding the child always rest with the parents.
☐ Always ask before assuming anything.
☐ Mother and father are to be consulted before taking action.
☐ Affirm the parents to and in front of their children.

There are always exceptions. Sometimes, out of default, grandparents become the primary caregivers or guardians, and then other rules apply. But grandparents normally provide an extended family role, which is to build up, support and provide a reprieve for harried parents. We can play a wonderful empowering role to this new family.

And Then There Were Teenagers

Our grandchildren's arrival in the teen years is another time in life when we can offer support to our families. We often have a capacity to relate to teenagers in a way their parents cannot. They can be more open to us about ideas that cause their parents to raise their eyebrows. When we take time to know our preteen and teenage grandchildren by being involved with them in various activities, we will have opportunity to share much of ourselves.

Last summer, for example, we (the Balswicks) received a great deal of pleasure in taking our grandsons with us on our vacation. The enthusiasm they, at ages ten and eleven, brought to the trip got us doing things and taking adventures we might not otherwise have attempted. We explored the West Coast together, crabbing at the ocean and fishing in the streams of Oregon, rollerblading the waterfront in Portland, taking the ferry to the San Juan Islands, watching salmon swim up the locks and enjoying many lakes in the Seattle area.

Jack's highlight was a kayak trip down the Rogue River, and my favorite time was telling stories at night. We have created a series of our own with Indiana Jake, Courageous Curt, Jewelry Judy and Jester Jack, who take all kinds of adventures together. It helps me understand how they think as we get into all kinds of predicaments in our stories and have to figure out how the Fearsome Foursome will overcome evil and fight for the truth. The Higher Power is always present to give advice and special words of wisdom about life.

So it seems we have come full cycle. We began writing this book about our teenagers growing up, leaving home and establishing lives of their own. Now we are living through that transition and moving into the role where we support our adult children all through these life stages.

What About Single Adults?
I (Boni) was recently working with a twenty-eight-year-old woman who was having difficulty relating to her parents. In an attempt to resolve things with them, she invited them to come to a therapy session with her. In the session she tried to explain how it felt to be twenty-eight years old and to be treated like a child. In the middle of her explanation her father interrupted her by saying, "Well, you are a child. You aren't even married yet!" Is that what it takes to qualify as an adult in our parents' eyes? For many, apparently so. But what an unfair burden we place on those who have been forced into, chosen or been gifted with singleness.

Not everybody gets married, but they certainly become adults. And single adults have a developmental process of stages that is unique to them. Since the thrust of our book deals with how parents relate to our adult children, we will focus on this aspect of single adulthood.

Significant Relationships

As we welcome a child's spouse into our household, we also welcome the friends of our adult children. Although adult singles may not have formed a family in the traditional sense, most have invested themselves in their work world and significant relationships. Their support group includes special friends, roommate(s), housemate(s), church and community connections. Their living arrangement may be permanent or transitory, but they have established themselves as adults in their given community. We need to show our support by acknowledging their achievements, maturity, choices and independent lifestyles.

Let your home be a place that offers hospitality to their friends and become adult friends with them. Honor their choices about singleness. Let your actions reflect your belief that singleness is a God-ordained way of being in our world. Rodney Clapp has devoted a chapter in *Families at the Crossroads* to "The Superiority of Singleness," in which he sums up his thoughts: "One sure sign of a defective interpretation of Christian family is that it denigrates and dishonors singleness" (Clapp 1993:113).

Our single adult children are most likely mature, independent adults who fully deserve our respect. Their life apart from us has a sacred boundary as well. We must not overstep it or wear out our welcome. We must not undermine them with stereotyped messages that suggest they are not adult until they marry or have children. We must never try to coerce them in any way. We include them in our family celebrations and appreciate their contribution as a single member. They play essential roles as uncles and aunts, siblings and adult children that we acknowledge with thankful hearts. They are persons who make a unique offering to our lives, and we are to esteem them highly and let them know how grateful we are for them.

The Single Parent

Some of our single adult children will also be parents. This may have come with death, divorce, separation or never-married status. The stress on these young adults is enormous. Many are still transitioning from adolescence to adulthood. Others have been on their own for a time and recently find themselves in a different situation from what they anticipated. Some parents may hesitate to lend a hand, thinking their children must prove they can do it on their own. Others step in and attempt to take over the young parent's life. We believe neither of those options is helpful to this family.

Once again the opportunity to be a positive influence presents itself to us. We do not want to take over or take on the responsibility of a second family, but we can be available to help out in many ways. First, we must educate ourselves to the particular stresses of the single-parent home. We have just begun to understand the consequences of traumatic distress on our children and the grandchildren who suffer the loss at deep emotional levels. Many experts identify the first two years following loss of a spouse as a crisis period for children in the home. The intense emotional upset, economic hardship and necessary readjustments are disruptive and disheartening. Single parents have too little time, too few resources and too few dollars, which puts considerable strain on this family. The relentless overload puts emotional pressure on the parent along with the emotional ups and downs of all family members. Attachment and loyalty issues increase anxiety as children try to put the pieces together. It is usually a bewildering time for children, who are prone to express anger and worry about the future.

Children are resilient and usually make the needed adjustments, but some researchers indicate that we must pay more attention to children who grow up in single-parent homes. For instance, there is a general tendency for children of divorce to drop out of high school, marry during teenage years and get pregnant prior to marriage (Cherlin 1992).

It is a great challenge for us to figure out the best way to help alleviate some of this stress and loneliness, especially during those first two difficult years. When our daughter was divorced, my (Judy's) husband and I were able to help financially so our grandsons and daughter had a stable environment. This gave them a chance to remain in a familiar home, school and community, which was comforting. Jacque's full-time work in a daycare center meant the boys could be with her before and after school, keeping their connection close. She developed a support group of friends who could meet her emotional needs while she took on the extra load of single parenting.

We made it a point to visit (a six-hour drive from our home) as frequently as possible so we could give Jacque a break from parenting and stay involved as grandparents. This made up for some of the loss of not having a father in the home. As Jacque worked through emotional stress, established herself financially and was doing well on her own, we became less involved in a helping role. We stayed close as parents and grandparents but acknowledged her independence and accomplishment as a single parent. We kept a clear boundary around her role as head of household and parent and honored her decisions. For us the best way to empower was to respect and love our daughter and her children.

Our place as grandparents is one we cherish. We have received the rewards and blessings in our mutually interdependent relationships.

Making Alternative Choices

We are aware that children reared by Christian parents do not always choose to follow Christ themselves. It is a reality that as our children grow, they must at some point claim Christ personally. Our faith may not be their faith. The child who never grasps Christ personally, who never submits to Jesus as Lord and Savior, will drift away from God and from God's teachings. The pain of watching this happen is excruciating. As these children leave Christ, Christian principles often go as well. This leaves new challenges for the parents as they try to find a way to relate lovingly to their young adult who has made other choices.

Cohabiting

In the United States, living together before marriage or in place of marriage is becoming as common as dating. Many young adults have never considered how this decision is contrary to scriptural principles. Many professing Christians have not grasped the reality that Clapp talks about. He reminds us that Christians have "the freedom to acknowledge and live within limits" (Clapp 1993:111). Our world does not like limits. We tend to look for ways to break them down rather than find the courage to live within them. As a result many young adults, not wanting to limit themselves sexually and not ready to marry, choose to cohabit. They have not faced the challenge of what it means to make a covenant before God that promises a lifelong commitment to their partner in marriage. Most fall into a cohabiting relationship out of convenience and mutual desire for a monogamous sexual union. Christian parents are often confused as to how to respond to such a decision. We see some parents ignore it as if it is insignificant and others who disown their children when they make this choice. It is important that we try to clarify how parents find a godly way to respond to this choice.

What makes the issue of cohabitation so painful for most parents? Watching our children deliberately choose their way and disregard God's way is a very hard thing for us to handle. It is especially hard when we feel there is nothing we can do but stand and watch. We hang on to any assurance we can find of a wandering son's or daughter's faith. It reassures us to see signs of faith in their kindness toward others or when they indicate their openness to God. When a child's profession of faith is unclear, we are eager to give meaning to small sparks that might indicate a growing desire in our child to follow Christ. We grasp at little signs and wrestle with the indicators of disbelief. When a child moves in with a partner, we have a hard time maintaining our hope. We begin to believe they have lost their faith and will never return to it.

Of course, this is true for any sin in our own lives as well. Our salvation in Christ is intricately tied to our obedience in Christ, and yet we know that salvation is based on what Christ has done for us rather than what we do on our own behalf. But as we choose our way over God's way, we hear the voice of Christ say, "My sheep hear my voice, and they follow me." Knowing that we hear him and follow him gives us assurance that we are his. When people, Christian or not, hear Christ's voice but choose to turn away from that voice, they deliberately put themselves in a vulnerable position. The blessings of God are dependent on our following God's way. This is why it is extremely hard for us when our children cohabit.

The important question for us as parents is how we are to respond to our children when they make choices that are not in accord with what we consider to be God's way for them. The only answer from our point of view is to continue to show the love of Christ to them. Whether it is the neighbor down the street or our firstborn son or daughter, we must show them the love of Christ and pray for their surrender to him. We must show love to their partner as well, rather than hating, blaming or conspiring to get rid of him or her. If we do that, we are missing the point. The fact that they have chosen a life that is contrary to God's way, not the person they choose to live with, is the issue. We cannot ignore their choice or pretend it is not happening, even when we are tempted to hide it from those at church who would not approve.

Perhaps another reason their choice to live together is so difficult for us is that it cannot be easily hidden. Our friends ask questions. Others make comments. We sense the issue is being talked about in church circles. We feel a loss of respect from peers who think we should do something about it. It is so blatant an action, and it unnerves us. But perhaps this is our sin of pride raising its ugly head. Who are we thinking about? Is it our children or ourselves?

It is hard to separate our reputation from that of our child. It is hard to remind ourselves that this is about them, not about us. But they are adults, and that is what we need to do. They have made this choice, and it is their choice, not ours. It is a good time to practice boundary setting, as discussed earlier. When family members make comments, direct them to your child. It is their issue to defend, not yours. You do not need to cover for them to Grandma or explain them to your pastor. Part of the boundaries that will be good for each of you is to know that this is their decision, not yours, and thus you can stay out of it.

The Gay Couple

What if the live-in partner is a person of the same sex? Does the issue change? We do not think so. The issue remains the same. Your child is refusing to submit to Christ. You would do best to treat him or her as you would other nonbelievers that God lays on your heart. Show your child compassion and kindness. Show Christ's love in all that you do.

A friend told me of her son's homosexuality and her feelings of being ostracized by people in her church. The Christians in her small group seemed to be of one mind: she should cut him off. Yet that did not seem right to her. "He knows I disagree with what he is doing. He knows I do not condone it. But he is my son. Shouldn't I show him the same love I try to show my unbelieving friends? Why would it be different?" We do not think it is. Always we need to keep the way open for our children's way back to Christ. Cutting them off will do just the opposite. Who can love them better than we can? By staying in contact, showing Christ's love and being interested in them as people, we let them know how important they are to us. It is not their behavior but them that we accept. Sharing Christ's love is always right. Keeping the name of Christ before them through our loving behavior is the least we can do.

It will most likely be even harder thinking of relating to the partner of this same-sex couple. Yet that is the situation you may be facing. Many parents can get to the point of relating to their own child but resist inviting the partner over. Perhaps they blame the partner for what is going on with their child, thinking their child has been negatively influenced by the desires and behavior of the other. Maybe that is out of a need to see our child as the more innocent one. Certainly much prayer will be needed to determine your level of involvement with the partner of your child. But in not inviting the partner home, you risk alienation from your son or daughter. We must ask God for the strength to love both our children and their partners in order that they will feel the love of God through us.

How Shall We Then Live?

As parents of mature adults who have made a variety of lifestyle choices, we must also choose how to live without our children. In a sense we become a re-formed family ourselves. At least for some of us it tends to feel that way.

For some couples this is an exuberant time of life. They take great joy in the freedom of being on their own again. There is no one to answer to except our partner. We can even stay out late without calling home or checking in with our kids. We seem to have more money to spend on things we never could do before. We have done our job, and now we are fancy-free. One couple we know said, "What leaves the house never comes back in the house." They meant the baggage their children take away with them, not the children themselves. However, it was understood there would be no boomerang children either. We may have more time to support our children, but we do it on our own time, not at their demand. No longer responsible in the same way, these parents have more enthusiasm to be involved in creative ways with their adult children and their families and friends. It is a delightful time of life, and there is much pleasure in making a life of their own and/or as a couple.

For other couples it may feel quite different. It may be a scary time to know how to be with one's spouse again without the children serving as a buffer. If you have typically related through triangles, it will be a challenge to relate in more direct ways. If you have failed to work out new patterns of relating, this can be a huge shakeup for the marriage. A season of depression and grief is a common response in these situations.

Perhaps the biggest challenge for parents now is to determine how they want their lives and/or marriages to be. Taking time to work this out, whether it be in therapy, an ongoing support group or a series of enrichment workshops, is the key. How we can make our marriages stronger and learn to compose our lives together in meaningful ways as a couple are tasks for married parents. How to continue life as a single person is the task for the single parent. We need to be intentional and move toward renewal in our lives.

We will do this for two different reasons. First, it is the task God has put before us. It is the stage of life we find ourselves in and a task we want to do in the most God-honoring way we can. Some married couples can never make the transition back to a couple. They fear being alone with their spouse and find other people or tasks to fill the gap so they do not have to face their partner. But this too is a task to be tackled and to learn to do well.

Another reason we face the challenge of living our lives well is for our children's sake. As they see us going on with our lives, they will be free to proceed with theirs. Parents who refuse to grow in their children's absence give the message that life without them is too difficult. This can make it hard for adult children to feel the freedom to grow and to be happy in their adult lives. The guilt of our unhappiness and discontent will carry over to the new families our children have formed. That is an unfair burden to put on them.

Develop a new family boundary now that your children have their own families. Imagine a circle around your spouse and yourself or around yourself if you are single. Imagine the pain and pressures of your present life within that circle. Imagine the joys and delights there too. You will choose to allow others into the emotional workings of you as a family from time to time. You will deliberately allow a break in the circle to talk over a problem with your friend or one of your children. But that will be a chosen action. You will contain your emotions, concerns and joys within your circle until you choose to do otherwise. And this is how it should be.

Without the circle around the new family left by grown children, we might tend to let all our pain spill over into our adult children's lives. They would be encumbered by how hard it is for us to live without them, how difficult it is not having anyone to talk to, how lonely it is and how our purpose for living seems to be gone. That is not their task. That is our task to figure out and to move on. We are not done yet; we have more learning to do that promises great rewards. Thinking in terms of that boundary circle may help you do that. God is in the middle of that circle, inviting you to find yourself and your meaning in Christ.

As we see, there are many choices our children have in how they live their adult lives. We have many choices in how we relate to them and their choices as well as how we re-form our family without them. As always, our task is to bring glory to Christ through our behavior. Sometimes that will be easily and cheerfully done. At other times it will be a challenge we would rather leave undone. Yet it is there for us. God is not done with us yet, nor is the Lord done with our children. As we learn to express the love of Christ to those around us, we hope to demonstrate a way to live as godly persons. We will not do it perfectly, but with God as our guide, our strength and our comfort, we will be headed in the right direction.

Exercise
Look at what is happening between you and your adult children at this stage of life. Is there anything you want to do differently so they have a more positive view of God's love for them?

11

Letting Go in Both Directions

....

Someone has said that children and old people need to be loved more than those in between. That often seems to be true. Those of us who try to love our elderly parents and at the same time show loving respect to our young adult children often feel the pressure of attempting to meet many demands from those on both ends of the continuum, and we wonder if we are doing anything well.

About the time we successfully launch our children, many of us begin caring for aging parents. This can be a difficult period for many of us as we let go of one generation and feel the pressure to take on another. This midlife time brings with it incredible pressures and responsibilities. It is a shock for many of us when we first begin to notice the signs of decline in our parents. Faltering health, insecurities about the future, unsteady steps, slips in memory and poor judgment in driving are some of the noticeable changes that seem to happen almost overnight. Many of us have been so busy launching our children that we are taken by surprise when our elderly parents begin to lean on us for help.

A Child No More

Most of us fool ourselves into thinking that our parents will be available to help us forever. A picture planted in my (Judy's) memory is the predictable day during any one of our visits to my in-laws when Jack's father would announce, "It's time to wash the cars!" At fifty years old, Jack would go into his little-boy role, scrubbing the cars under Orville's close supervision. Hose in hand and clearly in charge of the event, my father-in-law would give the instructions while Jack obediently went through the actions. So often when we return to the family we grew up in, we regress to the role of the young son or daughter. Our parents are in charge, just as they were in charge when we were children. Until now, that is. Something feels radically wrong when these familiar roles are reversed. The magical thinking is over and our fantasy is dispelled, for our parents have become frail and dependent. We become their caretakers. It is a shift we can resist no longer.

It seems they degenerate before our eyes. It gripped Jane's heart the day she realized that her father was no longer able to manage his finances. A good provider throughout the family's life, he now is confused by the simple task of writing out the monthly bills. David remembers how pitiful it was when his mother groped for the right words to say after her stroke. It was frustrating to them both when she was no longer able to make herself understood. A deep sadness passes through us and anger surges inside, for we want to denounce what is happening to them. Our strong parents have become weak, and when this comes we begin to prepare ourselves for the task of caring for and saying goodby to them.

Tying Up Loose Ends

Many of us have loose ends and unfinished business to face with our aging parents. When we begin to see the frailness overtaking them, we realize that we are facing one of our final opportunities to work out our relationships with our parents. We may have many losses to grieve or hurts to forgive or thanksgiving to express to our parents while they can still hear it. We gather strength to love unconditionally, and we are glad for times of intimacy that come from the vulnerability of their last days. We must say goodby to the way things were and meet the challenge of the new day.

Some of us have had a rare and priceless relationship with our parent(s). Many of us remember how they were by our side when we gave birth to those same children who have just left our homes. We were comforted and supported during the deepest losses and difficulties of our lives. They came to our rescue with wisdom and hope when we needed them. For others the relationship was a troubled and tormented one, which makes this caretaking role even more conflictual. Having had parents we never felt were there for us makes it difficult to lovingly commit to a caretaking role. Whatever the case, the stress of losing our parents is intense.

Too Much to Handle

The strain of caring for our elderly parents can be overwhelming at times, especially when it coincides with our adult children's leaving home. Then there are the other midlife losses that complicate things further. Facing such areas as our own physical changes, fading hopes and dreams, health concerns, career changes, financial difficulty or divorce makes this period a painful life transition for many. We feel that we have no more to give, and this added responsibility of caring for parents sometimes pushes us over the edge.

We question our capacity to be loving; we wonder whether we will have the energy or strength or patience to meet this final letting go. We worry that no one will relieve us when we are weary. We feel selfish when we consider the inconvenience and cost (personal and financial) of caring for our parents. Will we have enough time, how will it affect our marriage and family life, will our careers or jobs be jeopardized? If the debilitating illnesses of our parents tend to overstretch our abilities, we may face overwhelming guilt when we put them in a nursing home where they can receive around-the-clock nursing care. But this is the time of their life when they need us, and these are responsibilities we cannot shirk. Whether loyalty or guilt pushes us forward, we reach for the inner resources that make possible the personal sacrifices.

What Goes Around Comes Around

Taking care of our parents at the end of their lives reminds many of us of the sacrifices they made for us at the beginning of our lives. This can be a soothing reminder to us when things get particularly rough. Still, caring for parents can be one of the most trying times in our life. Sometimes our elderly parents can be extremely difficult to handle. They may have become cynical and grouchy with age. They can be stubborn and less than gracious as we attempt to help. We try to regard them with respect and consideration when we make decisions, but sometimes they are unreasonable and unable to think with clarity. We often give a lot without getting much in return, just as we did for our young children.

Making a conscious choice to be involved in the lives of our elderly parents at the end of their lives means we must anticipate how to do this with integrity and love. This is especially important when the relationship with our parents historically has been strained. We will need to search out resources in our community and allow family and friends to aid us in this challenging task lest we burn out and become resentful. Taking care of ourselves while taking care of our parent(s) is the best way to counteract discouragement and defeat.

Gerry certainly felt defeated when her ninety-year-old mother, Edith, pointed an accusing finger at her and said, "You don't know the meaning of love." Having her mother live with her at home had been no easy decision. But Gerry had never realized how hard it would be to sit under her mother's negativity and critical spirit. Evidently Gerry's decision to go to the mission field right after college had been viewed as a disloyal act of abandonment. After all those years Edith was venting her resentment over this past decision, overwhelming Gerry with guilt. Edith was not going to give her daughter an easy time. Taking care of Edith became a battle of wills over every little thing. Edith refused to take baths, ignored the clean clothes set out each morning and picked at the food Gerry prepared for her each day.

Things got more difficult day by day as Edith seemed to be winning a private battle but losing a relationship war. The ordeal of caring for her was much harder than Gerry had ever imagined. It is painful to be your mother's mother when, like a child, she rebels at every point. The worst times were the sharp silences and glaring stares. Ugly statements pushed Gerry's buttons until she found herself tempted to scream back at Edith. Feeling hopeless, Gerry began to doubt that she really did love her mother. Only through the loving support of her church community was she able to continue.

The morning Gerry found her mother dead, sitting in her chair with all her clothes on, she breathed a sigh of relief and said a word of thanks that she had persevered and had been able to finish caring for her mother. Gerry gently placed a blanket around her mother and grieved silently. There were few tears but a deep, inner sadness for her mother's unhappy life. Gerry was finally free and at peace, knowing she had done her best to care for her mother in a loving way. Though the rewards had been slim, knowing she made the last years of her mother's life as pleasant as possible gave Gerry assurance that the time she spent with her mother had not been wasted. God had given her the strength she needed.

Linda's decision to care for her elderly father was an especially hard one. Her father had sexually molested her in her childhood, and she had had little contact with him throughout her life. Just as her youngest son left for the navy, Linda received a call from a social worker telling her of her father's need. Many of Linda's friends and family knew the struggle she'd had in working through the effects of this abuse in her life. Unanimously they advised her to say no to this request. It was too much to ask of her, they thought. When God asks us to care for the elderly and to show respect for our parents, he surely did not mean this for Linda!

Yet Linda said yes to the request and took her father into her home to care for him in his last days. It was not easy to be loving and meet his needs. Yet it became a healing process for her. As she discovered her own strength in this situation, she found the capacity to forgive that had eluded her before. The experience was wonderful and awful. Linda says God used it for her growth like nothing else in her life.

Going beyond the call of duty can be done only through God's bigger love. We think Anna, a little girl, said it best when she was trying to grasp the difference between God's love and human love in a conversation she was having with her adult friend Fynn:

> "You love me because you are people. I love Mister God truly, but he don't love me. No," she went on, "no, he doesn't love me, not like you do, it's different, it's millions of times bigger. . . . Fynn, you can love better than any people that ever was, and so can I, can't I? But Mister God is different. You see, Fynn, people can only love outside and can only kiss outside, but Mister God can love you right inside, and Mister God can kiss you right inside, so it's different. Mister God ain't like us; we are a little bit like Mister God, but not much yet." (Fynn 1974:26-27)

Anna understood something special about God's love. If God's love is deep within us, we will be able to go the extra mile to love even when it is hard. God, our nurturing parent, knows our vulnerable insides, kisses and touches us deep where the hurt is. And God's love penetrates us to the core.

The Urgent Call

"It's time, Judy. You must come and do something about your dad *now*. The caretaker is overburdened being there for him day and night. She can't go on." My immediate response was "How can I drop everything at a moment's notice?" But the next day I am in Arizona making arrangements to put my father in a Christian nursing home. It is my crisis. It is our family crisis. My grown children have their busy lives to contend with and can do little more than offer compassion over the telephone. My mother grieves the fact that her beloved partner of sixty-five years is leaving their home; my dad is confused and anxious about the move; Elena, the caregiver, has a hard time not being emotional, for she feels bad that she can no longer handle the situation. Doctors are consulted, financial matters determined, family members notified, all within the matter of a few days. It is undeniably one of the hardest things I have ever had to do.

"The house is so empty since Dad is gone!" Now that Mom is back in her mobile home without Dad, she realizes she misses her lifelong companion more than she could have imagined. There is a dark and lonely feeling about the place. I wonder if it is going to be too much for her to handle. We talk about her feelings, and she admits, "I guess you don't know how much you miss a person until he's gone." Her sadness runs deep. I cannot change what is happening. I cannot take her hurt away, but I sense how much she needs me. I can be close and available to her as she asks, "Which one of us will die first, and who will be left behind?" Depression creeps in. We weep together, and our voices seem to echo the loneliness of the house. Sharing our vulnerability together is healing.

Did It Have to Come to This?
Dad (Judy's) was distraught and disoriented when we visited him. "Why am I in this place with all these crazy people?" he says. He tells of a woman calling for help and a man at the dinner table who slobbered all over himself. "When am I going home? I don't like it here. The bath is the worst part." On and on he goes. I think what he's saying beneath the words is "I'm afraid! I'm no longer in control." The small Bible on the stand next to his bed brings some comfort. Our prayers bring some peace. Christian music brings calm in the midst of the storm. And we make it through another night. We make it through another passage of life.

It is very difficult leaving our parents in situations where they do not feel comfortable. Sometimes the need of each of the parents is different, and we feel split between them as well as the needs of our immediate family. When my (Boni's) father became unable to care for himself, my mother was still an active person. She was eager for conversation, growth and activity. It was hard on her to be so limited in her life for so many years. Yet she was determined to care for my father as best she could, and she did her best. But we would often forget that she was seventy-six years old! Lifting him or caring for him hour after hour was too much for her at that age. We needed to provide care that took into consideration her limitations and her quality of life as well as the concern we all had for my father. That was hard to do when there were so many pressing expectations in each of our lives.

It is hard hearing the anguish in my father's voice as he tells me of his unhappiness. I feel torn as I think of his needs on one hand and struggle with the concerns of my daughter Sarah leaving home on the other. I feel so split inside. I am uncertain whose needs come first and where my energy should go. It feels like there is not enough energy to go around, not enough wisdom in me to meet the needs I see.

Is Everything in Order?

When parents lose control in physical and emotional ways, it is frightening. It is important for them to know that things are in order. It will help the situation greatly if some of this can be decided ahead of time. When our parents are feeling as if they are being stripped of all power, it is hard for them to give up the little control they have. If it is possible, talk these things through ahead of time. Help your parents decide who they want to be in charge when they are too weak to do it themselves. Let them discuss their priorities with you so you will understand what is important to them. Then when the time comes to take charge of the situation, you will have some guidelines to go by.

It can be hard to be the one in charge when the time comes to take greater responsibility for aging parents. I (Boni) have often heard people complain about the sibling in the family in charge of the parents. Since I live three thousand miles away from my parents, the task falls to my brother Chuck and his wife, Marianne. They are the ones who have to care for Dad when he falls or help Mom when she is exhausted from constant caretaking. So it seems natural that they should have the greatest voice in making decisions. They are our link to helping our parents. They know when more nursing care is needed, when another sibling needs to make an extra trip home or when financial help needs to be reevaluated. How easy it would be for me to sit on the other side of the country and tell everyone what to do. Yet the caretaker knows the situation and needs to have the authority to read the circumstances and make the judgment call.

I (Judy) had to reassure Dad that my brother and I would take care of his financial matters. Last year he struggled to get his income taxes done, but this year he does not have a clue where to start.

Mom wanted me to talk about her death plans. She had set aside her bright red blouse and white skirt to be buried in. She planned to leave her eyes to someone after she died. While I know there is no demand for her ninety-year-old eyes, blurred as they are with cataracts, this gesture touched me at a deep place. I remembered all the love I had received from those beautiful velvet-brown eyes.

Yes, Mom and Dad, everything is in order. We are in charge. We will see that it is done according to your wishes.

Making a Wise Decision

There are many things to consider before deciding to have aging parents move in with you. It is essential that you consider all the facts and details prior to making such a life-changing decision. One thing is certain: the lives of everyone will be changed by such a move. If a family is ill prepared, they can be flooded with feelings of frustration, guilt and despair. Even when the decision is made with the best of intentions, the daily reality is often harder than one ever anticipates, even though the rewards can also be far greater than one could imagine. Since your lives will be changed forever by such a move, it behooves you to ask some practical questions so you can make a wise choice.

Consider your own needs as well as the needs of your family or household. How will everyone be impacted (both positively and negatively) by your parents' presence? Take time for a brainstorming session with the family, indicating all the pluses and minuses for each family member and the family as a whole.

Consider the needs of your elderly parent as well as anticipate the negative and positive impact on them should they live with you. Write down the advantages and disadvantages for the parent.

What contributions will your parent make to the family and family members? Be specific about what they can do to feel useful and what would give them a satisfying and meaningful existence in your home.

Make a careful assessment of the physical, spiritual and mental status of the elderly parent and then ask if it is appropriate that you do the caretaking under these circumstances. For example, consider the level of dementia (feebleness of mind) and the continuing irreversible direction that is likely. Will the disruption be too severe for your particular family circumstances? Who will be most affected and how?

Ask yourself and your family members whether you can provide a caring, pleasant atmosphere in your home. Are you and your family equipped to be with your parent(s) through their emotional fears, confusion, agitation and childlike behavior?

Will your home be a secure and safe place for your parent? For example, are you willing to make necessary modifications to ensure wheelchair or walker access in your home (ramps, doorways, hallways, carpets) or do minor remodeling when it is necessary?

What level of care is needed? Can you afford to bring in skilled or nonskilled persons to help with the caretaking when you are away from home (at work, on vacations or trips)? Having a caretaker cook nutritional meals as well as take responsibility for basic hygiene and daily exercise will give you quality time for relationship connection and interaction. Careful planning will help you assess and anticipate the adjustments that will be necessary when you open up your home to your aging parent. The goal is to enhance the well-being of the whole person as a unique and special addition to your household.

Each person in the family, including yourself, is entitled to time and resources. The family is a wonderful resource and should not be exhausted or burdened beyond reason. We need to consider the best interests of all, because how we take care of ourselves, our marriage and our children is intricately interwoven in our ability to take care of our elderly parents. We cannot control our parents' lives, fulfill all their needs and produce happiness for them, but we can be responsible adult children, doing our best by being respectful, affirming our parents' worth and personality and preserving their dignity.

Be prepared to set up guidelines for you and your parents, similar to those we talked about in chapter nine. We must carefully attend to boundaries, clarity of expectations ("Please don't call me at night unless it's an emergency!"), dealing with differences, keeping communication lines open and working on building a relationship connection.

Some general guidelines for parent care are honesty (honestly sorting out sources of our feelings and limitations); integrity (doing what you believe is right for everyone concerned); fairness (exercising power through negotiation and compromise); respect (upholding a sense of dignity, autonomy, privacy, rights and interests of parents); and compassion (loving in ways that enhance the greatest positive good).

In order to ease the burden of parent care, we need to know ourselves, our parents and our family so we can rightly recognize our needs and our potential resources in living together. Making wise choices at this developmental stage of caring for elderly parents will have an impact on our adult children when they are challenged with caring for us in our old age. Just as we needed to trust God for our grown children, now we need to trust God for our elderly parents. God loves them, and we take comfort in knowing they are in ultimately in God's good hands.

You Have Limits Too!

If you are caring for an ailing parent, you are likely torn among the needs of your immediate family, the need of your parent and your own needs. Some aspects feel manageable, and others seem to overwhelm you. Yet it is important to accept both your limits and the limits of your immediate family.

Attempt to do the caretaking as a family if that is possible. Find out if your adult children are willing to be involved. Also, find out how they feel about your involvement in their grandparents' lives. Are they glad you can offer help, or do they feel it will detract from their needs? Are they able to accept your limitations of energy and strength? How can you work together on it?

Look at your relationship to your partner also. Are you able to reserve time for the two of you? How can you maintain a sense of partnership in the midst of midcycle challenges as opposed to losing each other in the process? Be sure to give this relationship the priority it needs.

Cultivate relationships that allow you to express what is going on inside of you. Is there someone in your life who can listen to your feelings of loss? Are you able to share your grief and doubts with a trusted person?

These simple considerations will help you stay clear about your priorities and the demands made of you during this time. If you know what is going on inside you, you will have a greater capacity to give care with love and compassion.

When Time Runs Out

Loving involves letting go of those we love. We have already learned this in relation to our adult children; now we are asked to do the same for our parents at their impending death. There is freedom in being able to say goodby to this life and each other. It empowers those we love to face their future and death with courage and dignity. By sharing our emotions and thoughts in the vulnerability of this time, we invite them to share their thoughts and feelings with us.

Frank was able to experience this in the months preceding and following his father's death. Having been off to college and then medical school, Frank had not been able to spend much time in his hometown since his late teens. Then his father learned that he was in the last stages of prostate cancer.

Immediately Frank was able to transfer to a hospital facility closer to home, which allowed him to more easily care for his father in his last days. By summer Samuel was confined to his bed, but his mind remained sharp. During many long, cool evenings, Frank and Samuel would talk—initially not about much other than his medical status, treatment options and related information, as this type of communication came easily for Frank. But as the reality of his terminal illness settled in, Samuel began asking his son more pointed questions. Sensing his son's fear of being honest, he explained that he knew he was dying and wanted his son to help him get things in order; Frank's honesty would help Samuel gauge his time frame. Frank explained that he was in the final stages and treatment now could only help keep him comfortable.

Suddenly those late-night conversations began to shift toward being more intimate, more reflective. Frank affectionately calls them his father's goodby talks. Most of the time Samuel needed his son to listen as he reflected on his life, how richly God had blessed him, how he could not wait to kneel before Jesus and kiss his feet for giving him both life on earth and eternal life in heaven. Frank remembered all those times when his father would glance at his wall calendar, which always depicted an image of Christ's resurrection. Daily Samuel would pause to give thanks and praise to Jesus for all that he had done. He looked forward to meeting his Creator face to face. Samuel's life as an immigrant to the United States had been hard, yet his face shone with gratitude that overwhelmed him to tears.

It was a wonderful time that deepened the understanding each had for the other. But then a greater joy yet occurred for Frank. Samuel began to focus on Frank, and at first Frank became a little uneasy. Frank had always had a good relationship with his father, but they did not talk much, not the way Frank had been able to talk with his mother, who had passed on many years before. Samuel was a man of few words. While Frank knew his father loved him, tinges of doubt used to surface from time to time. And in his father's silences Frank had often wondered if his father was proud of him. He interpreted his father's silence as disapproval and doubt about Frank's abilities. Despite being a gifted doctor, Frank often questioned his competence. Now he was about to hear his father explain the meaning of those silences.

To his surprise, Frank had it all wrong. His father chuckled as he recalled events from Frank's life from childhood though high school. Frank was shocked that his father had paid such close attention to his life. As was second nature for Frank, he muttered some self-deprecating comment about what the future held for him. Immediately fury rose up within Samuel as he took his son by the shoulders. Looking him square in the face, he scolded Frank for saying something so cruel about himself when God had blessed him with an abundance of talent, skill and intelligence. He went on to affirm that Frank could do anything he put his mind to and that all God required of him was to honor God by making the most of what he had been given.

Frank sat in stunned silence. He never knew his father felt that way about him. Later Frank told his father how touched he was by his comments. He then summoned the courage to tell his father that he wished he could have shared that with him when he was younger. Having never realized that Frank doubted his belief in him, Samuel was willing to talk with Frank about his concerns. In a long and painful conversation, Samuel came to understand the effects of his silence while Frank discovered the words of love and support that were spoken in his father's actions.

A few weeks later Samuel began to deteriorate. Frank felt helpless. All he could do was hold his father and be with him until the end. Frank did that, giving himself lots of time to rethink the relationship he'd had with his father all those years. It was a healing time for him and allowed him to feel the presence of his father in his soul throughout the rest of his life.

Our Fear of Death

It is not easy to watch our parents fail and eventually die. We realize we are not in control of this final phase of life. We acknowledge that part of our family life has come to an end. The old generation moves on, the next one lines up; then come our children and their children after them.

Many of us are not comfortable talking about our own death. Certainly Gerry's mother was not able to be as vulnerable as Judy's parents or Frank's parents were. We must honor their limits, as this is part of affirming their right to choose. But sometimes our own discomfort sends out a message that states death is an off-limits topic. Our loved ones pick up the signals and avoid the topic out of respect for us.

This fear is natural. Often it protects us from the reality that our parents are leaving. Sometimes it protects us from the reality of our own death someday. Compounding these deep emotional challenges is the fact that we live in a culture that encourages us to hide our grief and deny our mortality, leaving us with limited role models on how to deal with this stage of family life.

If you find yourself unable to give a family member the freedom to express his or her thoughts and concerns, you are not alone. But it is a significant block to overcome. Death is as much a part of life as growing up. It is a definite, predictable part of our individual and family life cycles. By embracing this stage—not looking the other way, not keeping the topic off-limits—we find deep intimacy that infuses our life with richness and meaning.

This year my siblings and I (Judy) have become closer as we have joined forces to take care of our parents. Sitting together around the dining-room table going through Mother's memory shoebox brought strength. Sorting through the cards and handwritten notes she had kept from her children, grandchildren and great-grandchildren, along with her hand-written sentiments, brought smiles. Reading her instructions about who should sing what songs at her funeral brought sadness. These private moments of reflection brought us closer during a difficult time of life. Through this family crisis of loving and letting go, we have taken more time for love and connection.

As we have said many times throughout this book, investing ourselves in those we hold precious is what life and death are about. We do not need to suffer in silence or as those who have no hope. Our family comes together again, young and old, to face life's toughest challenge: a final leaving home of one of our dear members.

Coming Full Circle

In Ecclesiastes 3 we are reminded that life is full of cycles, that life is about change and that it calls for us to recognize the place of each season within the grand scheme of things. "For everything there is a season, and a time for every matter under heaven: a time to be born, and a time to die; . . . a time to weep, and a time to laugh; . . . a time to embrace" and a time to let go (Eccl 3:1-2, 4, 5).

Our family's life cycle is full of changing seasons, of weeping and laughing, of building up and letting go. And within the cycles of our lives, within our pain and joy, God reveals to us but a part of the mystery of life. Happiness and sadness, triumph and tragedy are inseparable. All of these characterize the human experience. We hope that your family eagerly embraces each season of life with all of its wonder, beauty, sadness and challenge. And as you engage in the fullness of life, know that God is standing by your side waiting to lend an ear and lighten your load, eager to inspire you with energy and hope, providing a lantern to light your way in the name of his Son, Jesus.

Sometimes we feel we fail our children, and sometimes we feel we fail our parents. We try so hard to be good parents to our children and now parents to our parents. With our whole heart we try to love them enough to keep them safe and happy. We suffer with them and for them. We learn to give up and let go. Both grown children and elderly parents need us to see them through. They need our gentle guidance, our insight, our love and our acceptance, given with strength and humility.

Praise God for the model he gives us in God's Son, Jesus. And praise him for the Holy Spirit, who equips us to be like Jesus during these difficult times of letting go. May you feel the power available to you as you make the transitions before you.

Exercises

If you are caring for an ailing parent, specify what aspects feel manageable and what causes you concern. In whom do you confide when you are weary?

What specific things do you do to maintain a sense of partnership in these midlife challenges? List three things you would like to receive from that person(s). Be bold enough to ask for what you need.

Ask God to give you a deeper understanding of his love and purpose in this particular leg of life's journey.

Bibliography

Anderson, Herbert, and Kenneth Mitchell. 1993. *Leaving Home.* Louisville, Ky.: Westminster John Knox.

Balswick, Jack, and Judith K. Balswick. 1989. *The Family: A Christian Perspective of the Contemporary Home.* Grand Rapids, Mich.: Baker Book House.

Balswick, Judith K., and Boni Piper. 1995. *Life Ties: Cultivating Relationships That Make Life Worth Living.* Downers Grove, Ill.: InterVarsity Press.

Bowen, Murray. 1978. *Family Therapy in Clinical Practice.* New York: Aronson.

Buechner, Frederick. 1980. *Godric.* San Francisco: HarperCollins.

————. 1982. *The Sacred Journey.* San Francisco: HarperCollins.

Carlin, Lewis John, dir. 1979. *The Great Santini.* Orion Pictures.

Cherlin, Andrew J. 1992. *Marriage, Divorce, Remarriage.* Cambridge, Mass.: Harvard University Press.

Chodorow, Nancy. 1978. *The Reproduction of Mothering.* Berkeley: University of California Press.

Clapp, Rodney. 1993. *Families at the Crossroads.* Downers Grove, Ill.: InterVarsity Press.

Cocola, Nancy Wasserman, and Arlene Modica Matthews. 1992. *How to Manage Your Mother.* New York: Simon & Schuster.

Fynn. 1974. *Mister God, This Is Anna.* New York: Ballantine.

Kauffman, Gershen. 1985. *Shame: The Art of Caring.* Rochester, Vt.: Schenkman.

Keillor, Garrison. 1987. *Leaving Home: A Collection of Lake Wobegon Stories.* Harrisonburg, Va.: Donnelley & Sons.

Nouwen, Henri J. M. 1975. *Reaching Out: The Three Movements of the Spiritual Life.* New York: Doubleday.

Olson, David. 1986. "Circumplex Model VII: Validation Studies and FACES III." *Journal of Family Process* 25 (September): 339.

Potok, Chaim. 1972. *My Name Is Asher Lev.* Greenwich, Conn.: Fawcett.

Stein, Joseph. 1964. *Fiddler on the Roof.* Based on Sholom Aleichem's stories. New York: Crown.

Whitaker, Carl A., and William Bumberry. 1988. *Dancing with the Family.* New York: Brunner-Mazel.